P9-BAT-575

ASIA

INDIAN OCEAN

AUSTRALIA

THE BEST IN
TRAVEL PROMISE

Where is the best place to visit right now?

This is the most hotly contested topic at Lonely Planet and dominates more conversations than any other. As self-confessed travel geeks, our staff collectively rack up hundreds of thousands of miles each year, exploring almost every destination on the planet in the process.

Where is the best place to visit right now? We ask everyone at Lonely Planet, from our authors and editors all the way to our online family of bloggers and tweeters. And each year they come up with hundreds of places that are buzzy right now, offer new things for travellers to see or do, or are criminally overlooked and underrated.

Amid fierce debate, the list is whittled down by our panel of travel experts to just 10 countries, 10 regions and 10 cities. Each is chosen for its topicality, unique experiences and 'wow' factor. We don't just report on the trends, we set them – helping you get there before the crowds do.

Put simply, what remains in the pages that follow is the cream of this year's travel picks, courtesy of Lonely Planet: 10 countries, 10 regions, 10 cities and a host of travel lists to inspire you to explore for yourself.

So what are you waiting for?

28

66

114

CONTENTS

162

195

LONELY PLANET'S

TOP 10
COUNTRIES

Chile / South Korea / Portugal / Djibouti / New Zealand

Malta / Georgia / Mauritius / China / South Africa

Andean flamingos in the otherworldly landscape of Chile's Salar de Atacama salt flats

01

CHILE

█████ Chile is a sinewy sliver of a nation, isolated from the rest of South America (and indeed the world) by the soaring Andes to the east, the vast Pacific Ocean to the west, the bone-dry Atacama Desert up north and the impenetrable wilds of Patagonia down south. From its disparate extremes to the ever-trendier capital of Santiago at its heart, the country's citizens will unite in 2018 to mark 200 years of independence. Thanks to new non-stop flights from both London and Melbourne, it's never been easier to catch a plane, raise a glass of pisco sour and toast the celebration.

Population: 18 million

Capital: Santiago

Language: Spanish

Unit of currency: Chilean peso

How to get there: Chile's main international airport in Santiago receives flights from across the Americas, as well as a growing number of destinations in Europe and Australasia. Alternatively, buses link Santiago with cities in neighbouring Argentina, Peru and Bolivia.

TELL ME MORE...

Underappreciated Santiago has blossomed into a gourmand's playground in recent years as award-winning chefs use endemic produce to redefine Chilean cuisine. The capital city is also rivalling Buenos Aires with a flourishing performing arts scene that is set to expand in 2018 with the debut of a new 1880-seat Grand Hall at Centro Gabriela Mistral. But it's the coastal city of Valparaíso that continues to win the hearts of free-spirited travellers with its art-filled streets, bohemian cafes and romance-inducing promenades. In between these two cultural powerhouses you'll find the emerald-green vines of Casablanca Valley, whose wineries are increasingly tourist-friendly with walk-up tastings and tours. Of course, it's Chile's dazzling extremities that lure most travellers. Down in Patagonia, Puerto Natales got a newly expanded airport in late 2016, making the famed 'W' trek through Torres del Paine National Park more accessible than ever before. Up in the Atacama there's been a big bang in astrotourism, with new stargazing hotels and geektastic tours to groundbreaking observatories.

The colourful historic centre of Valparaíso, Chile's bohemian port that's long been a magnet for artists

SERJIO74 © SHUTTERSTOCK

ITINERARY
Two weeks in Chile

Ride the new state-of-the-art cable cars to the top of **Cerro San Cristóbal** to bask in sweeping views of Santiago beneath the snow-capped Andes.

Explore the playful mind of Nobel Prize–winning poet Pablo Neruda at **La Sebastiana**, his eccentric Valparaíso home.

Make historic **Casa Silva** vineyard your first stop on a tour of Colchagua Valley's stately wineries.

Relax weary bones in the sprawling **Termas Geométricas** thermal bath complex after a hike in the volcano-studded resort town of Pucón.

Ride a boat through **Laguna San Rafael National Park**'s foggy fjords to get up close to San Rafael Glacier, part of the sprawling Patagonian Ice Field.

La Sebastiana ② ① Cerro San Cristóbal
Casa Silva ③
Termas Geométricas ④
Laguna San Rafael National Park ⑤

UNMISSABLE EXPERIENCES

• Hike the five-day 'W' trek through Torres del Paine National Park, a highlights reel of Patagonia that can be as rustic (tents and camp grub) or chic (room and board *refugios*) as you want it to be.

• Become an amateur archaeologist as you amble past the mind-boggling *moai* statues of Easter Island, a remote Chilean territory in Polynesia that's shrouded in mystery.

• Use the oasis of San Pedro de Atacama as a base to visit the flamingo-filled lagoons, puffing volcanoes, ancient petroglyphs and high-altitude geyser fields of the world's driest non-polar desert.

'Chile used to sell the brand more than the land, but we've put the focus back on the land now because it's the most important thing when you're producing high-quality wines.'
Andrés Sánchez, winemaker at Viña Gillmore

TIME YOUR VISIT

Central Chile is a year-round destination, though heavier winter precipitation can put a dampener on plans (unless you're skiing in the Andes). Weather in the Atacama Desert doesn't change significantly from month to month, while Patagonia is best visited between November and March as many businesses (and trekking routes) close out of season.

• By Mark Johanson

The Paine River wends its way from the towering Paine Massif in Torres del Paine National Park, a major natural draw of Chilean Patagonia

SOUTH KOREA

South Korea is a compact playground of Asian modernity. High-rises soar in the futuristic capital city, Seoul, which in 2017 received a huge facelift with the opening of its new Seoullo 7017, a high-line park with cafes, bars and libraries along a disused elevated highway. South Korea has embraced its hosting of the 2018 Winter Olympics in Pyeongchang, and a new high-speed railway line will whisk travellers across the country to the Games. So don your hats and gloves to cheer on the best and brightest as they swoosh their way to glory. Or wait until it warms up and experience mountainous delights followed by steamy urban nightlife.

USCHOOLS © GETTY IMAGES

02

The traditional rubs up against the futuristic in South Korea's capital, Seoul

Population:	51.3 million
Capital:	Seoul
Language:	Korean
Unit of currency:	Won

How to get there: Most travellers arrive in South Korea on international flights to Seoul's Incheon International Airport. South Korea is also linked to Japan, China and Russia via ferries from either Busan, Incheon or Donghae.

TELL ME MORE...

Olympic year or not, South Korea is an unsung outdoor wonderland. You can hike up peaks that seem plucked straight from a scroll painting or raft on pristine rivers, while along 2400km of coastline you can surf, swim and sunbathe on sandy beaches. The urban centres of Seoul and Busan are packed with high-tech delights and quirky cultural pursuits, including a growing contemporary and street art scene, craft beer and spirits. Yet South Korea remains a country rich in traditional culture, where you can get a breath of Zen on an overnight stay in a peaceful temple or uncover history at Joseon-era palaces. The country's annual calendar is packed, from wintry ice festivals to glamorous film events with the stars. And South Korea's extensive bullet train network makes getting around easy: in 2017 a non-stop high-speed train service opened, connecting Seoul to Busan faster than you can fly.

> 'South Korea has so much passionate struggle and emerging creativity – you can't help but fall in love with the place.'
>
> *Hahna Yoon, writer and Seoulite*

ITINERARY
Two weeks in South Korea

- Take in **Seoul's** ancient palaces, markets and incredible food scene, including a day trip to the Demilitarised Zone to understand the complex history between South Korea and its northern neighbour.
- Head inland to **Seoraksan National Park** for mountain hikes, temples and hot springs.
- Learn about South Korea's rich history in **Gyeongju,** home to royal tombs from the Silla dynasty (57 BC–935 AD) and incredibly well-preserved ancient pagodas and pavilions.
- Finish on Korea's largest island, **Jeju-do,** for a wander up a lava rock-rimmed crater and the chance to taste seafood caught in the traditional way by female free-divers.

MARK DAFFEY © GETTY IMAGES

The changing of the guard ceremony at Seoul's Deoksugung Palace can be witnessed thrice daily

UNMISSABLE EXPERIENCES

• Those wanting a taste of traditional Korean life should take a stroll through a *hanok* neighbourhood. Twisting alleyways lined by these low-slung, slate-roofed houses are found all over the country, many of them transformed into artisan workshops, teahouses, craft *soju* (rice wine) distilleries and guesthouses with *ondol* (heated wooden floors).

• South Korea is nothing if not a food-obsessed nation, the epicentre of which is Seoul's chaotic Gwangjang Market, where vendors sling bowls of *bibimbap* (rice and vegetables) and sizzle up crispy seafood pancakes alongside more adventurous options such as pig's trotters, all washed down with milky *makgeolli* (unfiltered rice wine).

TIME YOUR VISIT

Spring cherry blossoms and autumn colours are a divine backdrop to outdoor pursuits, while South Korea's beaches delight in summer. The 2018 Winter Olympics will be held from 9 to 25 February, but even if you didn't manage to snag tickets, you can ski and snowboard on fabulous pistes all winter.

• By Megan Eaves

03

Sintra's hilltop Castle of the Moors was constructed in the 8th and 9th centuries

TOP 10 COUNTRIES

PORTUGAL

██████ **Portugal has emerged** from the long shadow cast by neighbouring Spain, seizing the spotlight as a dynamic centre for art, culture and cuisine. A spate of artfully designed museums have opened in the past two years, there's now a celebrated microbrewery scene, and rock-star Portuguese chefs are creating culinary buzz from Lisbon to the glittering beaches of the Algarve (seven new restaurants received Michelin stars in 2017). Heightening Portugal's appeal are its incredible affordability and its natural wonders: in 2016, more than 300 beaches earned the coveted Blue Flag rating and two new biosphere reserves were named. It's no surprise everyone is talking about this small, seafaring nation.

Population: 10.8 million	
Capital: Lisbon	
Language: Portuguese	
Unit of currency: Euro	

How to get there: Lisbon, Porto and Faro are Portugal's three international airports, with flights to Europe and North America.

TELL ME MORE...

Portugal straddles two worlds. Even on a short visit here, you can explore both its age-old traditions (classic cooking, vineyards, Baroque architecture), and its embrace of the cutting-edge – from open-air avant-garde graffiti galleries to nightlife driven by performance art. The adventure starts in Portugal's capital, with strolls along Lisbon's revitalised waterfront, meals at sprawling food markets (like the Time Out Market Lisboa in Caís do Sodré) and candlelit evenings listening to soulful *fado* at tiny nightspots in the Alfama. Afterwards, leave some time for wandering medieval clifftop towns (Marvão, Óbidos, Monsanto), beach-hopping along the coast, and urban explorations in Porto, an equally captivating riverside city in the north. There are architectural treasures and Unesco World Heritage sites, magnificent Roman ruins and wine routes criss-crossing the country.

'**What I love about Portugal is its unpolished, off-the-radar old-world charm. It manages to remain deeply authentic amid this globalised and heavily trampled world around us.**'

Kevin Raub, travel writer and Lisbon-based expat

HLPHOTO © SHUTTERSTOCK

Seafood cataplana, named after the copper pot in which it's cooked, is a classic Algarve dish

ITINERARY
10 Days in Portugal

- Begin in picturesque **Porto**. Wander historic Ribeira, admire the decadent Igreja de São Francisco and catch a concert in Rem Koolhaas' Casa da Música.
- Experience the culinary renaissance in **Lisbon**. Dine at Belcanto, a Michelin two-starred restaurant run by José Avillez, one of Portugal's best chefs.
- Delve into the past in **Évora's** atmospheric centre, home to medieval churches, a maze-like former Moorish quarter and a grand Roman temple.
- Continue down to the **Algarve** to explore some of the country's prettiest beaches.
- Finish in **Sagres**, a cliffside town perched on the edge of Europe.

Given Portugal's compact size and excellent road network, you can squeeze a lot into a single visit (though, of course, one visit is never enough).

UNMISSABLE EXPERIENCES

- Sip your way through the wineries of the Douro Valley, the world's oldest demarcated wine region. You can take vineyard tours and sample the great produce in tasting rooms, but it's well worth overnighting in a guesthouse on a wine estate, such as Quinta Nova or Quinta do Vallado.
- Wander through misty, forest-covered hillsides around Sintra, before visiting the surreal Quinta da Regaleira. The gardens surrounding this palatial villa are full of surprises, including a nine-tiered well, accessible via secret passageways. Sintra is also famed for its sinfully good pastries: try a *queijada*, with marzipan-like cheese filling.

TIME YOUR VISIT

Summer is the liveliest time to visit, with multi-day street parties in Lisbon and Porto. It's also the best time to enjoy those beaches (outside of June to September, the water can be bracing). Travel in April or May for springtime flowers and cooler temperatures – perfect for walks in the countryside. And in May, expect Eurovision fever to hit Lisbon, the host city for the outlandish annual song contest in 2018.

• By Regis St Louis

TOP 10 COUNTRIES

DJIBOUTI

� **Positioned for dramatic effect,** this petite nation is in the process of being ripped in three by diverging tectonic plates. Magma seethes beneath ever-thinning crust; Martian-like deserts spew steam from fumaroles; and sunken lake shores glisten with huge salt crystals. In geological terms, this is a sprint finish. But in human terms, this is spectacularly slow motion – a reason to make travel plans, not cancel them! Add intoxicating culture, beckoning beaches and incredible whale shark diving, and you have even more reasons to hop on a plane, or ride the brand new train, to witness Mother Nature at her brutal best in 2018.

ENDLESS TRAVELLER © SHUTTERSTOCK

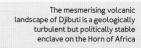
The mesmerising volcanic landscape of Djibuti is a geologically turbulent but politically stable enclave on the Horn of Africa

04

Population: 910,000

Capital: Djibouti City

Languages: Somali, Afar, French, Arabic

Unit of currency: Djibouti franc

How to get there: Djibouti-Ambouli Airport, 5km south of Djibouti City, welcomes a few dozen international flights a week. A new railway links the capital with Addis Ababa, Ethiopia.

TELL ME MORE...

Below the sea-line, Djibouti offers some truly compelling opportunities – and, incredibly, not all of them are under water. Venture down from the white-sand beaches to the crystal-encrusted shores of Lac Assal, a mesmerising crater lake surrounded by black volcanic hills – at 155m below sea level it's the lowest place in Africa.

At the other end of the country's spectrum are the Goda Mountains, which rise to a height of 1750m. Here you can trek through a relative oasis of green and absorb the charm of traditional Afar villages. Lac Abbé is another place for a stroll, but don't plan on making it far – you'll be constantly stopped in your tracks by the sci-fi landscape of spiky fumaroles bellowing out gases from the depths. Equally captivating are the Neolithic rock engravings at Abourma, which is a two-hour return hike over hills, along barren ridges and through vast expanses of chaotic boulders.

VUSLIMITED © GETTYIMAGES

Camel farmers haul palm tree leaves past Lake Assal, the lowest point on the African continent

> 'In a troubled region, Djibouti represents a haven of peace. From north to south, from east to west, we follow the same rhythm – everyone is welcoming and willing to help despite their limited means.'
>
> *Houmed Ali, Tour Operator, Agence Safar*

UNMISSABLE EXPERIENCES

Djibouti's exotic-sounding Bay of Ghoubbet, tucked at the western end of the Gulf of Tadjoura, is one of the world's most reliable sites to swim with whale-sized whale sharks. In some instances there are up to 10 of these giant fish moving close enough to shore that it's possible to snorkel out towards them. At other times they are further afield in the gulf and can be reached while on live-aboard dive boats. Ensure you book with an ethical operator that enforces ecologically sound guidelines, such as giving these majestic creatures a wide berth when in the water (at least 4m) and never allowing guests to get close enough to touch them.

TIME YOUR VISIT

The best – that is, coolest and most pleasant – months for exploration in this extreme desert landscape are November, December and January. Luckily for you, these months correspond with the arrival of whale sharks in the Gulf of Tadjoura. The waters are also calm for diving in October, and February through April.

• By Matt Phillips

ITINERARY
10 days in Djibouti

- Start in **Djibouti City** to soak up cultural vibes on the lively streets of the African and European quarters.
- Head west to **Lac Abbé**, where you can take in the sunset and sunrise over this alien landscape.
- Work your way back east to the baking depths and blindingly crystalline shores of **Lac Assal**.
- Continue to the nearby **Bay of Ghoubbet** for an unforgettable whale shark encounter.
- Move along the north side of the Gulf of Tadjoura for a multi-day trek in the **Goda Mountains** and a hike into the Abourma Rock Art Site.

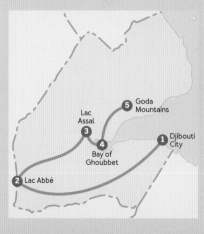

05

The curious limestone formations and blowholes in Paparoa National Park on the South Island were formed around 30 million years ago

NEW ZEALAND

Twenty-five years ago, long before it was retrofitted to resemble Middle-earth, New Zealand began actively attracting adventure-seekers. A sweet suite of trails, the Great Walks, encouraged exploration of the country's exquisite topography, taking tramping travellers through some of the world's most extraordinary wilderness. In 2018, for the first time since the nine-track network was launched, a new Great Walk opens: the Pike29 Memorial Track. This 45km route, which commemorates 29 miners killed in 2010, wends between Blackball and Punakaiki on the South Island's west coast, passing through Paparoa National Park, offering hikers and mountain bikers a sensational experience.

Population: 4.6 million
Capital: Wellington
Languages: English, Māori
Unit of currency: New Zealand dollar
How to get there: The country's major international airports are in Auckland and Wellington on the North Island; limited international routes also operate from Christchurch on the South Island. Regional and domestic flights arrive and depart from Queenstown and Dunedin (South Island). The Interislander Ferry connects the two islands several times daily.

TELL ME MORE...

New Zealand, teetering on the rim of the Pacific Ring of Fire, is a place where the planet's pulse pumps close to its scarred skin. Mud bubbles, mountains explode and glaciers melt into rivers rushing towards immense oceans, passing geothermally heated beaches. Here, the terrain remains undecided about its final form. Seemingly solid landscapes are torn asunder with a violence and unpredictability we don't expect in a country where cafes and pop-up bars serve artisan coffee and sublime craft beers on every urban corner. It's a wildly exciting place, where the best adventures are experienced under your own steam. The country is criss-crossed with quality trails, but there's a royal flush of routes – a premier league of paths that collectively caress the coast, clamber around the Southern Alps, explore escarpments, flow through Fiordland and venture onto the shoulders of volcanoes. These are the Great Walks. And now there are 10.

UNMISSABLE EXPERIENCES

• It's tough to top the Kepler, Milford and Routeburn tracks, or to ignore Tongariro's

ITINERARY
Two weeks in New Zealand

• Enjoy the urban scene in **Auckland,** the City of Sails, before heading southeast to Coromandel Peninsula's unique Hot Water Beach.

• Boggle at bubbly mud in sulphur-scented **Rotorua,** en route to Tongariro, where the one-day Alpine Crossing offers a taste of the Great Walk.

• From New Zealand's harbour-hugging capital, **Wellington,** catch the Interislander to **Nelson** and explore Abel Tasman's beaches.

• Drive super-scenic **Route 6,** diverting to walk the Pike29 Memorial Track and overnight in Moonlight Tops hut.

• Loop around **Aoraki/Mt Cook National Park** before wending through Haast Pass to **Queenstown.**

NARUEDOM YAEMPONGSA © SHUTTERSTOCK

Hiking past the 174m-high Earland Falls on the Routeburn Track, one of New Zealand's 10 Great Walks

lunar landscape, but the new Pike29 Memorial Track offers hikers and bikers a less trafficked experience along the South Island's wonderful west coast.

• Canoe to a campsite on the Whanganui River during a Great Walk that's actually a river journey and must be paddled from start to finish, or mountain bike the Heaphy Track during winter, when wheels are allowed.

• Watch sunset across Lake Waikaremoana from an eye-watering eyrie on the escarpment, or spy a shy kiwi bird while walking Stewart Island's Rakiura Track.

'The Great Walks perfectly encapsulate New Zealand's diversity – from Tongariro's steaming volcanic scree to Abel Tasman's golden beaches – and the addition of a 10th trail is monumentally exciting.'

Ben Southall, international adventurer

TIME YOUR VISIT

When tackling the Great Walks, timing is everything. In summer (December to February), competition for hut space can be as savage as New Zealand's blood-sucking sandflies, while winter can bring extreme conditions; use common sense and check weather reports before setting out. Spring and autumn are ideal. More relaxing out-of-season activities include star-gazing (Mackenzie), wine tasting (Marlborough) and hot-beach wallowing (Coromandel).

• By Pat Kinsella

The eighth wonder of the world?
Rudyard Kipling thought so:
Milford Sound, on the west coast
of New Zealand's South Island

MALTA

The long history of this Mediterranean **archipelago** is vividly evident. Prehistoric temples crown hills, 17th-century fortifications stalk the coast, and a warren of tunnels – from catacombs to air-raid shelters – dig deep underground. Its riches have been here for centuries, if not millennia, but Malta is experiencing a moment. This tiny nation's buzz has been building to a crescendo in preparation for Valletta's stint as European Capital of Culture for 2018. Expect baroque, pop and international film festivals, plus a contemporary art biennial. Not to mention a laid-back lifestyle born out of proximity to warm sea, beaches and more than 300 annual days of sunshine.

06

Attractively adorned Maltese townhouses line the streets of Valletta, a European Capital of Culture in 2018

Night falls on Victoria's medieval citadel on Malta's Gozo island

Population: 420,000

Capital: Valletta

Languages: Maltese, English

Unit of currency: Euro

How to get there: Malta International Airport has flights to and from all over Europe, as well as Dubai (via Cyprus). High-speed catamaran or regular ferry connections reach Sicily in a couple of hours, and Valletta is also a popular stop-off for cruise ships.

TELL ME MORE...

Ringed by cerulean water that sparks with silver-gold sunlight, the Maltese islands invite a dabble in watery pursuits, including some of the world's best diving. The sea gives a sense of endless space, with views onto the achingly blue horizon from, well... almost everywhere. In 2018, Malta's astounding cultural riches will be especially celebrated: the dripping-in-gold baroque-style St John's Co-Cathedral and Valletta's suitably named Grand Harbour will be backdrops for concerts and flotillas. In the run-up to the city's year as Capital of Culture, boutique hotels have opened in Valletta's lovely old townhouses and the local restaurant scene is ablaze with new openings. Yet there's so much that remains the same: the faded old bar signs on Strait Street (the former red-light district), the world's oldest record shop, jewellers selling candyfloss-fine Maltese filigree: for everything that is new, there are a thousand links with the past.

UNMISSABLE EXPERIENCES

• Eating a *pastizz* (warm pastry stuffed with ricotta cheese or spiced peas) fresh from the oven at Crystal Palace in Rabat. This hole-in-the-wall bakery offers Malta's finest version of the snack, as is clear from the queue of locals.

• Taking a dip in the Blue Lagoon, a beautiful sheltered cove with a white-sand seabed and

ITINERARY
A week in Malta

- Spend a day or two wandering around the treasures of capital city **Valletta**.
- Book ahead to visit the **Hypogeum**, a 5000-year-old underground structure, then dine in one of many coastal restaurants in St Julian's.
- Take a boat to the **Blue Grotto** and explore the nearby Ħaġar Qim and Mnajdra temples.
- Take it easy on soft sandy beaches at **Golden Bay** or **Għajn Tuffieħa**.
- Ramble the hilltop walled city of **Mdina** and neighbouring **Rabat**, then venture to Dingli Cliffs, Malta's highest point.
- Spend your last two days on **Gozo**, relaxing and exploring coves and red-sand bays.

'I love the sun! I love that I can get to the sea in a few minutes. We work hard, but you can stay home and feel you're on holiday!'

Denise Briffa, restaurant guide publicist

inviting, periwinkle-blue waters to explore.
- Walking to the clifftop prehistoric Ħaġar Qim and Mnajdra temples, and imagining how the heart-flipping views still looked the same 5000 years ago when the structures were built.

TIME YOUR VISIT
The Maltese climate is at its finest from April to June and September to October. July and August are baking hot and crowded, but also feature festivals and events. From November to March you'll enjoy more sunshine than in northern Europe, but weather is more erratic.
- By Abigail Blasi

The millennia-old cave city of Vardzia was home to about 50,000 people in its heyday. A few hundred monks remain in the cliffs today

GEORGIA

At this crossroads of the South Caucasus, history is not a thing of the past but informs every complex chess move Georgia makes in the present. Forward-thinking but proud of tradition, this is a country of ancient recipes cooked up in tucked-away taverns where toastmasters raise glasses of spirits to honour heroes old and new. It's so proud of its wine region that airport immigration officials often welcome travellers with a bottle of red along with their stamped passports. One hundred years ago, Georgia was declared an independent state in the wake of the Russian Revolution: just one of many reasons to raise a glass to toast 2018.

Population: 4.9 million

Capital: Tbilisi

Language: Georgian

Unit of currency: Lari

How to get there: An extensive network of buses, *marshrutky* (minibuses) and minivans connect Georgia with neighbouring countries and several destinations further afield. Tbilisi International Airport offers direct flights to and from almost 30 international destinations. Some regions remain off limits: check government advice before you travel.

TELL ME MORE...

Hemmed in by Russia, Turkey, Armenia and Azerbaijan, the influence of Georgia's eclectic neighbours is felt at every turn. Travellers adventure across the country's dramatic terrain, discovering Orthodox churches on soaring mountains, medieval monasteries tucked into green valleys, and cities carved into cliff faces. Visitors to these otherworldly sites leave mystified by the fact that the whole world isn't queuing for the experience, particularly given that nationals of many countries can travel visa-free for a whole year – and stunning bang-for-buck means they can afford to do so.

Wine has run through Georgian veins for the past 8000 years, with ancient methods still discernible in every drop today. Feasts

'Within hours of Tbilisi, with the Caucasus in striking white looming in the distance, there are still times you have a stunning landscape all for yourself, in absolute, complete silence.'

Marc Hulst, Tbilisi-based expat of 20 years

ITINERARY
Three weeks in Georgia

- Get culturally acclimatised in the cobblestoned Old Town of **Tbilisi** and day-trip to Davit Gareja for a glimpse of medieval monastic culture.

- Pick up the pace in **Batumi** to enjoy the incongruity of old-world seaside charm by the Black Sea, flanked by high-rises and party hot spots.

- Take on the wild trails of **Svaneti** that showcase picture-perfect alpine villages and snow-covered peaks.

- Up the altitude from **Kazbegi** by hiking through heart-stopping glaciers, waterfalls and mountain passes.

- Tuck yourself away in the epicentre of Georgia's epicurean pleasures, with a glass of wine among the vineyards of **Kakheti.**

of aubergine salad, spicy stews and fat, fresh *khinkali* (dumplings) are interspersed with rounds of lyrical toasts made by the *tamada* (toastmaster). Some foreign visitors have glasses raised in their honour and find themselves drawn into slurred singalongs with strangers...

UNMISSABLE EXPERIENCES

• Pressed against the Azerbaijani border, the remote desert caves of Davit Gareja comprise 15 monasteries carved into the hillside, adorned with detailed frescoes and murals.
• The medieval cave city of Vardzia, chiselled into a cliff face almost a thousand years ago, is both a portal to an ancient world and a functioning monastery today. Monks still inhabit some caves, meaning visitors must dress conservatively.
• En route to Russia, the easily accessible valley town of Kazbegi, silhouetting Tsminda Sameba Church against looming Mt Kazbek (5047m), is the launch point for walking, climbing or cycling the high Caucasus.

TIME YOUR VISIT

Thanks to world-class hiking, rafting and riding in summer and skiing in winter, Georgia is a year-round destination. When humidity is high in July and August, seek respite in the mountains or on the Black Sea coast. The Kakheti wine harvest runs from late September to late October.

• By Marika McAdam

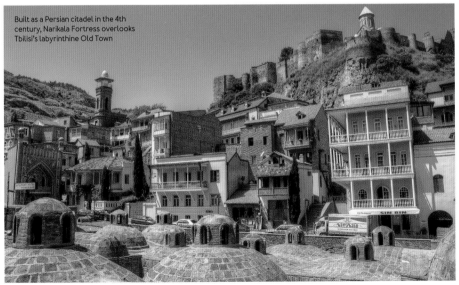

Built as a Persian citadel in the 4th century, Narikala Fortress overlooks Tbilisi's labyrinthine Old Town

High in the Caucasus, the Svanetian Towers were built as tribal defences over 1,000 years ago and now form a Unesco World Heritage site

MAURITIUS

This brochure-perfect island idyll is justly famous for its dazzling sapphire seas and luxurious beach resorts, where the watery fun includes coral reef dives, kitesurfing, sea kayaking and lagoon cruises. During the colonial days, Mauritius was known as the 'Star and Key of the Indian Ocean' for its strategic position. These days there's much afoot in the deep blue sky, with the government establishing the island as a hub for flights to mainland Africa. New connections to Mauritius include Air Mauritius and KLM's service from Amsterdam. Past glories are also getting a spotlight in 2018, when the island celebrates 50 years of independence.

A typically breathtaking
scene in Mauritius; the island
nation celebrates 50 years
of independence this year

08

Population: 1.4 million	
Capital: Port Louis	
Languages: Creole, Bhojpuri, French, English	
Unit of currency: Mauritian rupee	

How to get there: Carriers including Air Mauritius operate direct flights to Mauritius' Sir Seewoosagur Ramgoolam International Airport from Europe, Africa, the Middle East, Asia, Australia and beyond.

TELL ME MORE...

A good time to join the multicultural, mostly Creole and Indo-Mauritian islanders in celebrating their departure from British rule is around Independence Day (12 March), when the nation's flag is raised at Port Louis' Champ de Mars racecourse. The annual ceremony also features military parades, fly-pasts, live music and choreographed dance and light shows, while the flag's four colours adorn children's smiling faces at community events across the island. Expect eye-bulging spreads of curry-and-flatbread snack *dhal puri*, seafood from octopus salad to spicy fish *vindaye*, Creole classics such as *rougaille* stew, dim sum and, of course, pineapples, coconuts and rum punch. The diverse cuisine is a reflection of an island influenced by Dutch, French and

'**Mauritius is rich in history, cultural traditions and authentic experiences. Walk into Port Louis' lanes to discover its central market's diverse stalls, and explore the wild south of the island.**'
Amélie Marrier d'Unienville, tour guide

Chamarel Waterfall plunges more than 95m in a single drop

ALES-A © GETTY IMAGES

ITINERARY
Two weeks in Mauritius

• Mauritius' tourist hub **Grand Baie** has unbeatable shopping and party credentials. Base yourself in a neighbouring beach village.

• Explore *la côte sauvage* ('the wild coast'), as the island's exclusive eastern flank is known, while staying in **Trou d'Eau Douce** ('sweet water hole') with its nearby isle, Île aux Cerfs.

• Bucolic mountain hamlet **Chamarel** is a gateway to Black River Gorges National Park and the colour-banded sand dunes of the Terres des Sept Couleurs.

• Forested **Île aux Aigrettes,** 800m offshore, shows what Mauritius looked like when the first explorers arrived.

• A 90-minute flight leads to the remote Mauritian territory of **Rodrigues,** a volcanic outcrop surrounded by lagoon and coral reef.

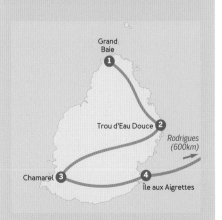

British occupation, and inhabited by the descendants of people who arrived with the trade winds. Equally, sights such as Triolet's 19th-century Hindu temple bear testament to this patchwork society, while myriad adventure activities prove that there is more to Mauritius than beaches.

UNMISSABLE EXPERIENCES

• Hike amid old-growth forests and waterfalls in the Black River Gorges National Park, home to the endemic Mauritius kestrel, pink pigeon and echo parakeet.

• Explore the 19th-century finery of plantation house Eureka, a Creole mansion fit for Cluedo with 109 doors and French East India Company furniture, and the Italian neoclassical-style Château de Labourdonnais, where tropical orchards and a rum distillery complement the sober Victorian furnishings.

• Seek out the mountainous hinterland on adventure tours such as electric mountain-biking to the 100m Chamarel Waterfall and an old sugar factory with Electro-Bike Discovery, and zip-lining down forested gorges at Casela World of Adventures.

TIME YOUR VISIT

The tropical climate makes Mauritius a year-round destination, with warm and dry winters (May to November) and humid summers (December to April). The early months of the year see rainfall and cyclones, and the trade winds can be too breezy in July and August. Christmas is busy but good for diving.

• By James Bainbridge

The Great Wall of China

09

CHINA

The world's most populous country is big, beautiful and full of mystery and adventure. Since 2016, China has opened extensive new high-speed rail tracks, creating the largest HSR network on Earth. Běijīng's imperial palace – the Forbidden City – has been upgraded in the past few years, and four previously restricted halls are now open to the public. Gargantuan Shanghai Tower welcomes visitors to the world's highest observation deck, and in late 2017, cultural hub Design Society opened in the cosmopolitan city of Shenzhen, featuring a partnership gallery with London's V&A Museum. Twenty-first century China is here to stay, so hop on board a bullet train and explore this modern Middle Kingdom.

CHINA

Population: 1.3 billion
Capital: Běijīng
Languages: Mandarin Chinese, Cantonese, Portuguese (Macau), English (Hong Kong)
Unit of currency: Yuan Renminbi
How to get there: International flights arrive into all of China's major cities; Běijīng and Shanghai are the main hubs. The Trans-Mongolian Railway connects Běijīng to the Trans-Siberian Railway and Moscow through Mongolia.

TELL ME MORE...

The stunning sights scattered across China's vast territory are no secret. You can uncover ancient civilisations, explore gleaming megacities, hike the iconic Great Wall, gaze up at starry Silk Road skies and see some of the world's most profound Buddhist art. Once far-flung destinations like Silk Road jewel Gansu and backpacker outpost Yunnan in the southwest have suddenly become more accessible on speedy new rail lines. Even public toilets have smartened up, thanks to a recent 'toilet revolution'. Glass bridges were constructed at warp speed over the past two years, giving visitors a new vantage point over spectacular forested ravines. Key sights have been spruced up, including a state-of-the-art visitor centre for the Buddhist treasure-trove at the Mogao Grottoes, a refurbished ancient town in Datong and even a craft beer trail across southern China on the glitzy new Shanghai–Kunming high-speed train.

UNMISSABLE EXPERIENCES

• Taking in the 'golden triangle' of China's mega-sights: walking on the Great Wall, feeling very small in Tiananmen Square, seeing the

ITINERARY
One month in China

● Start in **Běijīng** to see the Forbidden City and Summer Palace, and day-trip to Mutianyu to walk up the Great Wall.

● Jump on a speedy train to laid-back **Xi'an** to see the Army of Terracotta Warriors and get to know China's Islamic heritage.

● Take in **Shanghai**'s cityscape from the world's highest observation platform and enjoy the leafy French Concession.

● Head into the countryside for an unforgettable sunset over the **Yuanyang Rice Terraces** in Yunnan province.

● Finish in non-stop **Hong Kong.** Don't miss an evening ride on the Star Ferry, the view from Victoria Peak and a cocktail or three in edgy Sai Ying Pun.

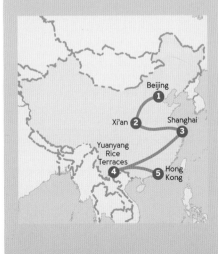

EDWIN REMSBERG © GETTY IMAGES

'I am always drawn to Běijīng's hutongs. A coffee at Cafe Zarah, then brunch on the rooftop of the Orchid Hotel, followed by a cycle around Houhai Lake.'

Carl Setzer, founder and owner of Great Leap Brewing

A man rides his bike in a hutong located in Central Běijīng

vast Army of Terracotta Warriors in Xi'an and gawping at the blazing neon skyline of Shanghai.
• Scoffing freshly fried noodles or steaming dumplings at a night market, crispy sliced duck at Dadong Roast Duck in Běijīng or dim sum at one of Hong Kong's age-old teahouses.
• Travelling the ancient Silk Road to gaze up at giant Buddha statues, walk the inner *kora* (pilgrim path) at Labrang Monastery and sand-sled down peach-coloured dunes.

TIME YOUR VISIT

Spring and autumn are generally the best times to visit this vast country. Summer can bring heat and humidity to the south, and winter can be bitingly cold in the north. Chinese New Year falls on 16 February in 2018. Be aware that the 40-day travel period surrounding this holiday brings big crowds and ticket woes.

• By Megan Eaves

The ancient practice of cormorant fishing, where the bird catches fish too big to swallow, can still be witnessed in some parts of China

SOUTH AFRICA

Beaches and mountains, wildlife and wine, and let's not forget vibrant culture and cosmopolitan Cape Town – South Africa has long been one of the world's most alluring countries. This year the country's many attractions will be bolstered by 'Nelson Mandela Centenary 2018: Be the Legacy', an official programme of events – some sporting, some educational, others devoted to the arts – aimed at honouring the legendary leader. The theme is to inspire values-based societies, with exhibitions related to transparency, service, respect, passion and integrity. So with more to see than ever, and favourable exchange rates offering great value, 2018 is a phenomenal year to visit South Africa.

MHGALLERY © GETTY IMAGES / ISTOCKPHOTO

10

Cape buffalo are a common, if
intimidating, sight in South Africa's
wildlife-rich national parks

Population: 54 million

Capitals: Pretoria, Bloemfontein, Cape Town

Languages: Zulu, Xhosa, Afrikaans, English, Swati, Tsonga, Southern Sotho, Tswana, Venda, Northern Sotho, Ndebele

Unit of currency: South African rand

How to get there: Cape Town International Airport and Johannesburg's OR Tambo International Airport are the principal points of arrival for air travellers. Overland options include border crossings with Namibia, Botswana, Mozambique and Zimbabwe.

TELL ME MORE...

Crawling with iconic African wildlife, big and small, South Africa is a premier safari destination. But these adventurous forays into incredible wilderness cost a fraction of those elsewhere, as South Africa's national parks and reserves are priced for domestic visitors. The same can be said for some of Africa's most spectacular hiking choices, whether climbing craggy peaks in the 2430-sq-km uKhahlamba-Drakensberg Park, walking the coastal trails within Garden Route National Park or seeking out ancient rock art in the Cederberg Wilderness Area. Table Mountain is another outstanding place to stretch your legs, and the urban environment lapping its

'There's a complexity in how to see the world here. Intellectual complacency isn't tolerated. If you're engaging with fellow citizens, you're compelled to constantly re-evaluate your world view. I love that.'
Iain Harris, Founder, Coffeebeans Routes

The 300km Garden Route takes in such paradisiacal vistas as the beach at Wilderness

PETER UNGER © GETTY IMAGES / LONELY PLANET IMAGES

flanks – Cape Town – is rightly regarded as one of the world's most beautiful cities. Its diverse cultural delights, golden beaches and vineyards are all worth a trip in their own right. Even Johannesburg, a city once avoided by visitors, is now brimming with hip, thriving neighbourhoods such as Maboneng, Norwood and Braamfontein.

UNMISSABLE EXPERIENCES

• Embarking on a self-drive safari within the 19,485 sq km of unforgettable wilderness in Kruger National Park – wait at zebra crossings, pause for breath at rhino crashes and skirt carefully through the long shadows of elephants.

• Walking the remote Wild Coast from the Great Kei River to Port St Johns, where rugged cliffs, sandy beaches and rural Xhosa villages create a captivating journey.

• Delving into the troubling – and too recent – history of the country's past at the compelling Apartheid Museum in Johannesburg and on Robben Island, off Cape Town, where Nelson Mandela spent 18 of his 27 years in prison.

TIME YOUR VISIT

Safaris are amazing all year round, but the prime time to visit is June to September, as water is scarce and animals congregate around drinking sources. Summer weather (November to March) is ideal for all other pursuits. Visit in late August or early September to bathe in the colours of wildflower season.

• By Matt Phillips

ITINERARY
Two weeks in South Africa

Start in **Cape Town** with a hike (or cable car) up Table Mountain for incredible views, before chilling on a beach and dining in style.

Move east to whale watch in **Hermanus**, then continue along the scenic Garden Route to take in the forests and lagoon of **Knysna**.

After a flight to the port of Durban, head up into the **uKhahlamba-Drakensberg** for some enthralling hiking or submerge into the Indian Ocean to dive with sharks at **Protea Banks**.

Plug into the captivating inner-city vibe of **Johannesburg**'s up-and-coming neighbourhoods.

Fly into **Kruger National Park** to experience the majesty of South Africa's wildlife.

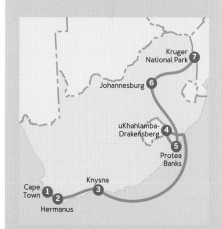

TOP 10 REGIONS

Belfast & the Causeway Coast, Northern Ireland / Alaska, USA

Julian Alps, Slovenia / Languedoc-Roussillon, France / Kii Peninsula,

Japan Aeolian Islands, Italy / The Deep South, USA / Lahaul & Spiti, India

Bahia, Brazil / Los Haitises National Park, Dominican Republic

North of Belfast, the Giant's Causeway in County Antrim is perhaps Ireland's most iconic attraction

01

BELFAST
& THE CAUSEWAY COAST, NORTHERN IRELAND

▬▬▬▬ **Belfast's transformation** over the past two decades has been remarkable. A city once patrolled by heavily armed troops and dogged by sectarian violence is now full of hip neighbourhoods that burst with bars, restaurants and venues to suit all tastes. The rusting old docklands are now the vibrant Titanic Quarter, home to fancy apartments and a sensational museum. Beyond lies the Causeway Coast, whose timeless beauty and high-grade distractions – golf, whiskey and some of the world's most famous rocks – are more popular now than ever.

61

Population: 280,000 (Belfast)

Main town: Belfast

Language: English

Unit of currency: Pound sterling

How to get there: Belfast's two airports are well served by direct flights from Britain and mainland Europe. Belfast Central train station serves Dublin and all destinations throughout Northern Ireland. The Causeway Coast is best reached by bus from the Europa Bus Centre or by car.

TELL ME MORE...

Belfast has much more to it than the legacy of the Troubles, though you should definitely visit Crumlin Road Gaol – a working prison until 1996 – to get a sense of how scary things became. Belfast is also the birthplace of the RMS *Titanic*. The Titanic Experience is an unmissable multimedia extravaganza that charts the history of Belfast and the creation of the world's most famous ocean liner. Close by, take a tour of the SS *Nomadic*, a steamship ferry built in 1911.

Along the Causeway Coast, the Giant's Causeway is the big attraction – but Harry's Shack in Portstewart is an altogether more earthy pleasure. Inside this National Trust–owned wooden shack is one of Northern Ireland's best restaurants, the perfect

'While the Giant's Causeway draws all the crowds, I'm just as happy with a knickerbocker glory at Morelli's in Portstewart – they've been there since 1911!'

Stephen McKenna, travel operator and Portstewart resident

ITINERARY
Two days in Belfast & the Causeway Coast

• Take a free tour of **Belfast City Hall**, a late-Victorian edifice whose grandeur is testament to the city's enormous wealth at the time.

• Explore the **Cathedral and Titanic quarters**, followed by drinks in one of the city's magnificent Victorian pubs, notably the Crown Liquor Saloon and the Duke of York.

• Head northwest to the **Giant's Causeway**, and clamber about its magical basalt columns before visiting the riveting Giant's Causeway Visitor Experience.

• Test your nerves by crossing the **Carrick-a-Rede Rope Bridge**, which spans the chasm between sea cliffs and a small island. *Game of Thrones* shooting locations pepper the area around, for example at nearby Ballintoy.

• Steady your nerves with a whiskey or more at **Bushmills Distillery**.

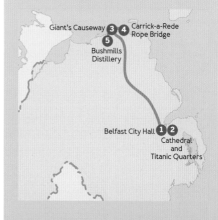

Giant's Causeway ❸ ❹ Carrick-a-Rede Rope Bridge
❺
Bushmills Distillery
Belfast City Hall ❶ ❷ Cathedral and Titanic Quarters

destination after a round of golf on the stunning Portstewart links; it's not as famous or as expensive as the links at Royal Portrush just down the coast, but it's every bit as beautiful.

UNMISSABLE EXPERIENCES

• Board a black taxi for a 90-minute tour of West Belfast's troubled political legacy. Black Taxi Tours – you can pick them up all over town – take you up the Catholic Falls Road and down the Protestant Shankill Road, past the famous murals and the infamous 'peace wall', the barrier originally erected in 1969 to separate the warring Catholic and Protestant communities of West Belfast.

• Explore Bushmills Distillery's giant copper stills and embrace the whiskey fog with a snifter of five different blends in the premium tasting room of the world's oldest legal distillery. Sleep it off in the adjoining inn.

TIME YOUR VISIT

Summer (June to August) is the most popular time to visit, when Ireland's unpredictable weather is usually at its best. But September often delivers long sunny days that stretch into the evenings. There are fewer crowds too, so you can enjoy the scenery in greater tranquillity.

• By Fionn Davenport

NAHLIK © SHUTTERSTOCK

Titanic Belfast's striking exterior houses exhibits exploring the famous ship and Belfast's industrial heritage

ALASKA, USA

Mixing incredible wildlife with a rough-and-tumble outdoor spirit, Alaska satisfies any thirst for adventure. Where else can you spend 20-hour summer days tackling snow-laden mountains, spotting grizzlies or following the path of the Klondike gold rush? Due to increased flight links to many North American and European cities, Alaska has never been easier to reach. Recently, the state's major cruise companies have announced expanded capacities, larger ships and more variety for travellers. Smaller operators like Alaskan Dream Cruises are increasing their itineraries and expeditions, too, allowing more options to spot bald eagles, humpback whales and glacier-studded fjords.

02

A magnificent humpback whale breaches the surface of the ocean against the Alaskan mountain backdrop of Glacier Bay

Population: 742,000
Main town: Anchorage
Language: English
Unit of currency: US dollar
How to get there: Ted Stevens Anchorage International Airport is Alaska's largest airport and serves several direct international flights. The Alaska Marine Highway System maintains a ferry route beginning in Bellingham, Washington, and winding through the Inside Passage. A popular overland trip is the Alcan (Alaska–Canada) Highway, via Yukon Territory in Canada.

TELL ME MORE...

Containing the country's largest national park (Wrangell-St Elias) and biggest state park (Wood-Tikchik), plus the tallest mountain in North America (Mt Denali), the vast, untrammelled wilderness of Alaska is speckled with awe-inducing natural features. Take a floatplane to a remote camp, where grizzlies far outnumber humans; buckle up for an 800km road trip into the Arctic tundra; or don crampons and hike across a glacier.

There's also plenty to experience in Alaska's towns and cities. Take the gold-rush town of Chicken (population: seven-ish). According to local lore, it gained its name because no one knew how to spell 'ptarmigan', the chicken-like bird that roams the area. Or there are the Alaska Native communities whose traditions have endured for millennia. Visit the remote Iñupiat town of Utqiagvik (formerly Barrow), where ancient and modern coexist. Wherever you go, the harsh landscapes and tough winters have yielded people with incredible stories.

Studying ice melt via SUP on Bear Lake in Kenai Fjords National Park

JAMES + COURTNEY FORTE © GETTY IMAGES | AURORA OPEN

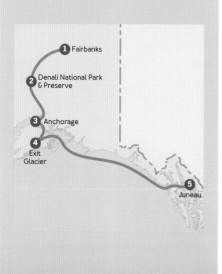

ITINERARY
Two weeks in Alaska

• Bask in the midnight sun or gawk at the Northern Lights that blaze over edge-of-the-wilderness **Fairbanks**.

• Explore the boreal forest and tundra of **Denali National Park & Preserve**.

• Feel refreshed by the city life of **Anchorage**, taking in the museums, galleries and restaurants that make it one of Alaska's most vibrant cities.

• Hike across **Exit Glacier**, Kenai Fjords National Park's signature attraction and just one of the 30-plus glaciers that dot the valleys around the Harding Icefield.

• Make your way to scenic **Juneau** aboard the Alaska Marine Highway System, keeping your eyes peeled for whales.

① Fairbanks

② Denali National Park & Preserve

③ Anchorage

④ Exit Glacier

⑤ Juneau

UNMISSABLE EXPERIENCES

• Mt Denali, the eponymous highlight of Denali National Park & Preserve, is a natural destination for travellers eager to experience the state's marvels. For many, it can be the sole reason to book that Alaska-bound flight. At 6190m, the mountain's sheer size makes for a once-in-a-lifetime encounter. But it's not just the granite monolith that makes Denali National Park worth the trip: Alaska almost certainly offers the world's best chances of seeing grizzlies, moose, caribou or (if you're lucky) a wolf. The most popular way to spot these beasts is through the window of the park's shuttle buses (summer only; reservations recommended).

'You'll realise Alaska is unique when you're staring into the night at the aurora pulsing overhead, and the lonesome howl of a wolf floats out of the great frozen silence of Arctic winter.'

Seth Kantner, commercial fisherman, writer and wildlife photographer

TIME YOUR VISIT

The high season runs from June through August, when hikers and wildlife-spotters can enjoy long days and solstice festivals are held throughout the state. Most people avoid winter, when temperatures can drop to -28°C in the state's interior. The Northern Lights begin to appear in September.

• By Alexander Howard

Atop a small island in the middle of Lake Bled, the baroque Church of the Assumption can be reached by traditional Slovenian *pletna* boat

03

JULIAN ALPS, SLOVENIA

With the natural appeal of Chamonix or Zermatt – but with fewer crowds – the Julian Alps offer mountain bliss in an overlooked corner of Europe. Over two-thirds of the region is protected by the Triglav National Park mandate, a mechanism that not only curbs development along the summits but ensures that improvements to local infrastructure are effected in a slow and studied manner. Once suitable only for the intrepid, the Julian Alps are gently opening the door to every stripe of traveller. A growing number of locally run operators are pairing pulse-racing treks with upmarket versions of homestays in stylish shepherd digs.

Population: 130,000
Main towns: Kranjska Gora (north), Bovec (southwest) and Bled (east)
Language: Slovenian
Unit of currency: Euro
How to get there: Slovenia's only international airport, Ljubljana Airport, is a 45-minute drive from Kranjska Gora or 25 minutes from tourist hub Bled. From Trieste and Venice airports in Italy, access the region via Bovec (allow 90 minutes to two hours by car). Public transportation is infrequent; it's worth hiring a car.

TELL ME MORE...

When Hollywood calls to film a fantasy flick on your home turf, you know you hold the keys to an ethereal realm that bests the top CGI artists in the industry. Locals in the Julian Alps are quick to point out that their backyards were featured in *The Chronicles of Narnia: Prince Caspian*, not to mention a slew of other European and even Bollywood films.

This kingdom of stone, unmarred by chair lifts wired to the western summits like guitar strings, is undoubtedly the initial draw for tourists. But it's the friendly locals that leave an indelible impression. Declared one of the top 10 most peaceful countries in the world by the Global Peace Index, Slovenia's citizens are eager to break bread with visitors, especially

'As a climber, mountaineer and guide, the Julian Alps are my playground, my school and my office all in one. A good grip of limestone in my native mountains will always be home to me.'
Aleš Česen, IFMGA mountain guide, Piolet d'Or winner

ITINERARY
A week in the Julian Alps

• Start with three days in **Triglav National Park**, climbing and hiking through the snowy ranges. Arrange a multi-day trek and sleep in mountain huts, or stay in the valleys for comfortable day walks.

• For rafting and kayaking, base yourself in tourist-friendly **Bovec** or smaller **Kobarid**, currently buzzing due to Hiša Franko, the local restaurant run by Ana Roš – featured on Netflix's *Chef's Table*.

• Enjoy quiet **Bohinj**, snapping the perfect picture of Mt Triglav's signature peak from Vogel ski resort.

• Finish in fairytale-like **Bled**, and take a *pletna* (think: gondola) to the church-topped island floating in the middle of its emerald lake.

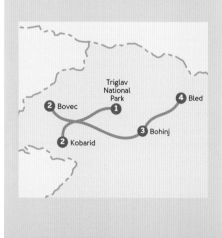

BARAT ROLAND © SHUTTERSTOCK

Skiing in the beautiful Julian Alps
can be a pocket-friendly pastime

in the Julian Alps where the land yields fresh farm-to-table meals, best paired with guided walks around protected lakes and silent peaks.

UNMISSABLE EXPERIENCES

• Ascending Slovenia's highest peak, Mt Triglav, is a rite of passage for adventurous locals. The average active traveller should allow two days to complete the trek with a registered mountain guide, spending the night in a hut towards the exposed summit.

• Slovenia's agrotourism offerings are vast. In the Julian Alps guests stay in quaint shepherd huts and feast on delicious cheeses and local cream cake (rather like a Slovenian millefeuille).

• Known as the green river, the Soča's pure waters glisten with an emerald tint. Raft past adorable villages after a few days climbing the region's signature stone towers.

TIME YOUR VISIT

Late August to mid-September, when tourist numbers dwindle, is an ideal time to take advantage of mountain hikes and warm inland lakes. Winter is a wonderland for adventurous climbers eager to battle the elements, for ski pros attempting record-setting jumps at Planica, or March's annual Ski World Cup event in Kranjska Gora.

• By Brandon Presser

Dusk falls over Lake Bled
and the mountains as
viewed from Ojstrica Hill

LANGUEDOC-ROUSSILLON, FRANCE

The charms of the south of France are many and varied: white beaches, blue seas, country markets, maquis-covered hills. But for too long, Provence and the Côte d'Azur have stolen the limelight, and 2018 might be the year that the lesser-known region of Languedoc-Roussillon takes its turn in the sun. Two swish new museums are currently in the works, and they're set to put this fiery corner of France on the map – although anyone who's tasted the region's fabulous food and fine wines really won't need any extra reasons to visit.

Above the Orb River in Béziers sits the fortified Saint-Nazaire cathedral, dating from the 13th century

04

Population: 2.7 million
Main town: Montpellier
Language: French
Unit of currency: Euro
How to get there: Toulouse is the main hub, with direct flights to the UK and most European cities.

TELL ME MORE...

Two millennia ago, Languedoc was part of the Gallo-Roman empire. The area is littered with Roman ruins, notably the fabulous Pont du Gard aqueduct and the well-preserved ruins of Nîmes and Narbonne. In 2018, the Musée de la Romanité opens in Nîmes, designed by Elizabeth and Christian de Portzamparc. It's a striking addition to a town that already has a Norman Foster-designed art gallery, and promises a new perspective on the region's Roman past.

Meanwhile, over in nearby Narbonne, Foster is currently hard at work on another museum, MuRéNa, exploring the town's own imperial history – although rumour suggests it might not be ready until 2019. No matter: Languedoc is awash with other attractions, from crumbling Cathar fortresses to the wild hills of the Cévennes, and fascinating towns like Perpignan, where rugby is an obsession and the big match blares out from every late-night bar.

UNMISSABLE EXPERIENCES

• Pretend you're Russell Crowe as you wander around the Roman amphitheatre in Nîmes, where gladiatorial battles and gruesome spectacles were once staged in front of 24,000 baying spectators.

Listed by Unesco, the Pont Du Gard aqueduct over the Gardon River is one of Languedoc-Roussillon's many Roman attractions.

'My tip for art-lovers is the Musée Fabre in Montpellier – it has an amazing collection including works by Rubens, Poussin, Manet and Degas, and it's not well known outside France!'

Sylvie Dubonnier, student in Montpellier

ITINERARY
A week in the Languedoc

● Start out in **Nîmes**, gazing out at the vast amphitheatre and venturing out to nearby Pont du Gard.

● Head west to **Montpellier**, home to sun-kissed beaches and grand medieval townhouses known as *hôtels particuliers*.

● Re-enact *Jurassic Park* at the kid-friendly **Parc des Dinosaures** in Mèze, where life-size models bring the giant lizards to life.

● Take a boat trip along France's most illustrious waterway, the **Canal du Midi**, from Béziers or Narbonne.

● Finish up in **Perpignan**, where French and Spanish cultures collide – it crackles with Catalan culture and is home to the former palace of the Kings of Majorca.

● Explore the battlements of the medieval city of Carcassonne, famous for its pointy turrets shaped like witch's hats. We defy you not to think of *Monty Python and The Holy Grail*...

● Spot wildlife and canoe down the canyons of the Parc National des Cévennes, a remote, forested region that's off the tour-bus radar.

TIME YOUR VISIT
It's hot here in summer – seriously hot – and many French people choose to take their summer holidays here during August. So this region is better explored in spring or autumn: May and September are great months to visit. In April, Nîmes stages Roman-themed games in the atmospheric setting of its amphitheatre.

● By Oliver Berry

1 Nîmes
Parc des Dinosaures 2 Montpellier
3
4 Canal du Midi
5 Perpignan

05

The Nachi waterfall cascades 133m beside the pagoda of the Seiganto-ji Buddhist temple

KII PENINSULA, JAPAN

Travel to Japan is red-hot. The number of visitors has doubled in the past three years and is only predicted to rise. Since the word is out about this thrilling country, travellers need to dig a little deeper. The Kii Peninsula, which dips down into the Pacific Ocean south of major tourist draws Kyoto and Osaka, offers many of Japan's most lauded attractions. There are Shintō shrines and Buddhist temples, sublime natural scenery and steaming hot springs, traditional culture and modern convenience – but without the crowds. So far, that is... the Kii Peninsula is starting to get noticed, in part because travelling here is remarkably hassle-free.

Population: 1 million (Wakayama prefecture)
Main town: Wakayama City
Language: Japanese
Unit of currency: Japanese yen
How to get there: The nearest airport, Kansai International Airport, has links from major Australian, European, Asian and west coast US cities. Coming from Tokyo or elsewhere in Japan, Osaka is the nearest city on the *shinkansen* (bullet train) network.

TELL ME MORE...

There are two factors that define the Kii Peninsula as a destination – its lush landscape and the surprising ease of travel. It's among the wettest places north of the tropics: the trees grow dense and tall, the air is thick and misty, and moss and lichen give the whole scene an otherworldly gravitas. It's no wonder that it has long been considered one of the most spiritual places in Japan. The temples and shrines have drawn pilgrims for centuries, particularly Kōyasan, a deep-in-the-mountains complex founded in the 9th century, and the wooden shrines (of similarly ancient pedigree) along the Kumano Kodō trails.

Getting around is easier than most other places in rural Japan, thanks to a number of savvy recent initiatives. Walking trails, expertly maintained, are now completely signposted in English. Detailed itineraries, maps and bus

'I like the Kogumodorigoe section of the Kumano Kodō. It sees few people, which means you can really hear the songs of the birds and the sounds of your own footsteps.'
Yamamoto Naoya, owner, Blue Sky Guesthouse on the Kumano Kodō

ITINERARY
A week in the Kii Peninsula

- Wander paths past mossy stupas on the way to **Oku-no-in**, Kōyasan's sacred hall, ensconced in a dramatic Buddhist cemetery.
- Cross from the ordinary world to the sacred one at **Takijiri-ōji**, the first of five major shrines on the Kumano Kodō and where your walking journey begins.
- Admire Kumano Hongū Taisha in **Hongū**; hewn of local cedar and sparingly adorned, it's a glorious example of traditional shrine architecture.
- Soothe your weary legs in **Yunomine Onsen**, one of Japan's oldest known hot springs.
- End your pilgrimage the traditional way, with a ride in a flat-bottomed rowboat down the Kumano-gawa to **Shingū**.

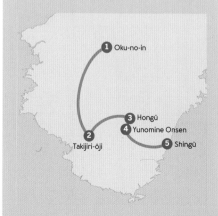

schedules are available in English online. A luggage-forwarding system means you can travel unencumbered.

UNMISSABLE EXPERIENCES

• Spend the night in a *shukubō*, lodgings run by a Buddhist temple. Kōyasan has dozens of them, where you sleep on futons on tatami (woven reed) mats and eat meals of *shōjin-ryōri*, vegetarian food prepared by Buddhist monks. Ekō-in is well set up for foreign travellers and guests are welcome to join meditation sessions.

• Walk the Kumano Kodō, one of two Unesco-listed pilgrimage routes (the other is Spain's Camino de Santiago). You can spend a day or a week on the trails, under a canopy of trees, following in the footsteps of 1000-plus years of spiritual seekers.

TIME YOUR VISIT

Spring and autumn are the best times to visit. Beware of rainy season (June to mid-July) and typhoon season (September), which can hit the Kii Peninsula hard. Summer is cooler here than most of Japan, though August has some scorchers (and a greater likelihood of crowds).

• By Rebecca Milner

© WAKAYAMA TOURISM FEDERATION

In the Kii region of Japan, centuries-old festivals and practices still endure

06

BEST IN TRAVEL 2018

TOP 10 REGIONS

AEOLIAN ISLANDS, ITALY

■■■■■ **Floating photogenically** in the Tyrrhenian Sea, a stone's throw off the tip of Italy's boot, the Aeolian Islands are a slow travel paradise. Shaped by their explosive geology, these seven alluring sisters woo visitors with sublime seascapes, volcanic slopes, black-sand beaches, and some of Europe's best coastal walks and dives. The islands have been largely off the beaten track, but their low-key charms have begun luring wise travellers seeking a good-value Mediterranean break. Even sleepy Alicudi, the Aeolians' remotest outpost, is having an influx of walking tourism, so 2018 may be your last chance to outpace the crowds.

MATT MUNRO © LONELY PLANET

Looking down the west coast of Lipari to Vulcano on the idyllic Aeolian archipelago

06

Population: 17,000
Main town: Lipari
Language: Italian
Unit of currency: Euro
How to get there: Regular ferries and hydrofoils link the Aeolians to Naples and the Sicilian ports of Milazzo and Messina.

TELL ME MORE...

Italians seeking sun and sand have long adored the Aeolians as a midsummer haven for *dolce far niente* (carefree idleness). More recently, a new wave of outsiders has begun to discover the islands' slow-paced appeal in the off-season. The entire archipelago abounds in gorgeous walks, from lazy meanders along flower-strewn shorelines to awe-inspiring treks up the active volcanoes of Stromboli and Vulcano. Neighbouring Salina and Panarea court a refined crowd with their wineries and family-run boutique hotels, while rustic Alicudi is a hermit's fantasy at the end of the ferry line, where steep mule paths climb from a torpid fishing port past vine-draped adobe houses to the island's lonely, dormant crater. The Aeolians' multilayered history comes alive in Filicudi's Bronze Age ruins or the Greco-Roman shipwreck troves and theatre masks at Lipari's archaeological museum. Meanwhile, island cuisine is universally fabulous: think pasta with swordfish, capers, wild fennel and mint, or the creamy-crunchy cannoli in every *pasticceria* window.

UNMISSABLE EXPERIENCES

• Nothing compares to a sunset climb up Stromboli, the Aeolian Islands' most charismatic volcano. A two-hour ascent brings you face-to-face with the fire-spewing crater, with the exquisite Tyrrhenian Sea sparkling 900m below.

'My magic spot is Pizzo dell'Osservatorio, a lava ridge that looks down over Vulcano, with Filicudi and Alicudi silhouetted against the setting sun. I sit here before nightfall and let time slip away.'

Marcello Giacomantonio, owner, B&B Al Salvatore di Lipari

Although its permanent population is only around 10,000, Lipari town is the main hub in the Aeolian Islands

- For an unforgettable beach day, trek down to pebbly Spiaggia Valle i Muria beneath Lipari's western cliffs. Between spots of sunbathing, sip drinks in Barni's beach cave bar then sail home through the sea stacks at twilight, with Vulcano smoking seductively on the horizon.
- For the ultimate Aeolian breakfast, grab a whipped cream-slathered lemon, coffee or pistachio *granita* (flavoured crushed ice) at Da Alfredo on the Lingua waterfront (Salina island).

TIME YOUR VISIT

The Aeolians are at their most delightful on either edge of peak summer season. Visit in May and June for brilliant hiking conditions, with long, generally sunny days and a profusion of wild flowers. For warm waters and ideal swimming conditions without the crazy August crowds, September is an unbeatable choice.

- By Gregor Clark

ITINERARY
A week in the Aeolian Islands

Acclimatise to island life in **Lipari**, the Aeolians' buzzing hub, where narrow alleys lead to picturesque waterfront cafes backed by an ancient citadel.

Hop over to **Vulcano** for therapeutic mud baths and a straightforward one-hour climb to the smouldering crater.

Set sail for **Salina**, a twin-coned beauty where you can sip locally grown Malvasia wine, swim beneath dramatic cliffs and stride through vineyards to verdant summits.

Lose yourself in the eternal romance of **Stromboli**, the Aeolians' hyperactive fire-breathing volcano, famous since antiquity for its near-constant eruptions.

Finish with a foray to the blissfully sleepy, oft-forgotten outer islands of **Filicudi** and **Alicudi**.

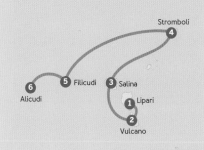

Iron-lace balconies are a familiar sight on Royal Street in New Orleans' French Quarter

THE DEEP SOUTH, USA

In 2018 it will be 50 years since Martin Luther King Jr was assassinated in Memphis, and the anniversary has spurred several civil rights-focused sights to open. Foremost is the Memorial to Peace and Justice in Montgomery, Alabama, a stunning structure of suspended columns that pays homage to the nation's 4000 documented lynching victims. King's birthplace in Atlanta is being refurbished for visitors, and the motel where he was killed – now transformed into the National Civil Rights Museum – is holding a year's worth of poetry slams, concerts and other special events. Meanwhile, New Orleans turns 300, and it's throwing a multi-event birthday party that'll carouse through the year.

Population: 34.5 million

Main town: Atlanta

Language: English

Unit of currency: US dollar

How to get there: Atlanta's Hartsfield-Jackson International is the region's (and the USA's) busiest airport. New Orleans also has a major airport, and its new, expanded terminal opens in 2018. Highway 61, the fabled Blues Highway, runs south through Memphis clasping the Mississippi River to New Orleans.

TELL ME MORE

The Deep South conjures visions of all sorts. It's the thick-column plantation homes with sweeping verandas in Georgia, and the long, low land of forsaken cotton fields in the Mississippi Delta. It's moss-slicked cypress trees and alligators floating in Louisiana's bayous. It's barbecue smoke drifting from a tumbledown shack in Alabama, where the pork ribs and lemon icebox pie might change your life.

'I love living here because every zydeco accordion blast, every perfect pecan pie, every lingering summer-night conversation is a reminder that who I am and where I am are inextricably linked.' *Michael Tisserand, New Orleans resident*

JOE DANIEL PRICE © GETTY IMAGES

Spanish moss draped over trees in Savannah, Georgia

ITINERARY
Two weeks in the Deep South

• Gnaw on barbecue, pay your respects to Elvis at Graceland and tour the haunting National Civil Rights Museum in **Memphis**.

• Follow the landscape of silent cotton fields to **Clarksdale**, Mississippi, the region's foremost town for blues history and blow-the-roof-off bands.

• Hear Dixieland jazz, consult with a voodoo priestess and spoon into thick, spicy gumbo in **New Orleans**.

• Poke around **Montgomery**, Alabama's sleepy capital, to see the Rosa Parks Museum, the new memorial to lynching victims and other social justice sights.

• Indulge in New South eats, swirl cocktails, check out art and wander in MLK's footsteps in mannerly **Atlanta**.

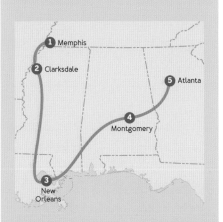

The region also flashes images of slavery and civil rights fights. The National Civil Rights Museum tells the story. It's at the Lorraine Motel, where Dr King died. The exhibits culminate at Room 306, preserved with empty dinner plates and ruffled beds, as it was the day King stepped out on the balcony and was shot – a time warp straight to the chilling moment. It's intense but illuminating, like the Deep South itself.

UNMISSABLE EXPERIENCES

• Ready your fork for plates of fried chicken and turnip greens, butter-smothered biscuits and flaky peach cobbler. New Orleans, Atlanta and Charleston are chowhound hubs, but any mom-and-pop diner will serve the region's pan-crisped, gravy-ladled staples.

• Saturday night at a bluesy juke joint or fast-fiddlin', accordion-pumped zydeco dance hall will knock your socks off. Truly. You think you'll stay in your seat, listening to the band howl on stage, but then the 40-ounce beers and twinkling lights work their magic and suddenly you're out there with everyone else, dancing up a sweat. The Mississippi Delta and Louisiana's Cajun Country are hot spots.

TIME YOUR VISIT

April and May are warm and lush. Summer is steamy, often unpleasantly so. Winter is generally mild and crowd-free. Mardi Gras, New Orleans' mega-bash, lets loose 13 February. Elvis Week brings fans to Memphis around the 16 August anniversary of his death.

• By Karla Zimmerman

Beautiful colours on old cypress trees reflected on the calm water of the swamplands just before sunrise.

LAHAUL & SPITI, INDIA

If you like your mountains big, your roads rugged and your landscapes verging on the supernatural, then the windswept valleys running east and west from Keylong are a little piece of Shangri-La. Kept bone-dry by the rain-shadow of the Himalaya, the ochre badlands of Spiti hide some of India's most spectacular Buddhist art, while well-watered Lahaul has seldom-visited temples and a back route to Kashmir said to be one of the world's most dangerous roads. Long overlooked by travellers rushing to Ladakh, this wild and wonderful area is finally starting to get the attention it deserves. Come now, before it becomes just another stop on the Himalayan 'apple pie' trail.

Dhankar Gompa, a Buddhist temple, balances atop a rocky cliff at an altitude of 3984m in the Spiti Valley

08

Population: 31,528

Main town: Kaza

Languages: Hindi, Lahuli-Spiti

Unit of currency: Rupee

How to get there: The only way into Lahaul and Spiti is by road, either north from Manali, south from Ladakh, or west from Kinnaur. The nearest airports are at Bhuntar, Leh and Shimla, and the mountain passes to the north and south are usually open from May to November.

TELL ME MORE...

On paper, Lahaul and Spiti look to be easy detours off the road to Ladakh – but in this torturous terrain, every journey is an expedition. Crossing into Spiti involves a breathless climb over the 4551m Kunzum La before you tumble into the parched valley of the Spiti River. Amazingly, this arid landscape supports pockets of life: scattered apple orchards, isolated Buddhist monasteries and tiny white-washed houses, stacked to the rafters with firewood to last through the long winters.

Heading west, explorers trade the badlands for deep, green valleys dotted with folk-art and Hindu temples, before embarking on the mortality-testing journey to Kishtwar in southern Kashmir, on a road that is little more than a score-line along sheer rock walls. There'll be moments when you wonder why you didn't head straight to Leh for a latte and massage, but then you'll catch sight of the impossible landscape and smile at the thought of how few travellers you have to share it with, for now...

UNMISSABLE EXPERIENCES

• Seeing the monochrome landscape burst into kaleidoscopic colour in the mural-

ITINERARY
A week in Lahaul & Spiti

• At first glance, Spiti's **Tabo Gompa** is a plain-looking congregation of geometric, mud-brick forms; inside is some of the most intricate and elegant Buddhist art in the Himalaya.

• The vertiginous views down over the Spiti Valley are even more impressive than the murals at ancient **Dhankar Gompa**, balanced precariously on a cliff wall in the Pin Valley.

• Spiti's largest Buddhist monastery, **Ki Gompa**, rises like a fortress over the floodplain north of Kaza.

• The rustic exterior of Lahaul's **Markula Devi Temple** hides another treasury of religious art – ancient wooden friezes carved with scenes from the *Ramayana* and *Mahabharata*.

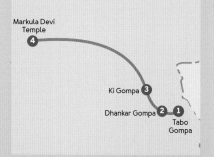

The mountains are alive with the sound of traditional instruments in Himachal Pradesh

08
BEST IN TRAVEL 2018

cloaked chapels of Tabo, which is the oldest continually operating Buddhist monastery in the Indian Himalaya.

• Sipping salty butter tea with cheerful novice monks at Ki Gompa, then sitting back to enjoy the morning *puja* – an uplifting cacophony of murmured *sutras* (scriptures), honking horns and clanging gongs.

'The ride from the Rohtang La to the Kunzum La has to be one of the world's most amazing adventure rides. The rock-strewn route is little more than a trekking trail.'

Amar Bodh, motorcycle tour company Dusty Trail Adventure

• Travelling the bone-shaking highway between Keylong and Kishtwar, carved in defiance of gravity into the bedrock of the Himalaya. Do you dare to travel one of the world's most dangerous roads?

TIME YOUR VISIT

The tourist season for Lahaul and Spiti is dictated by the weather. The Rohtang La (between Keylong and Manali) and the Taglang La (between Keylong and Leh) are iced over most winters from November to April. Snows can block the Kunzum La, dividing Lahaul and Spiti, from October to early June.

• By Joe Bindloss

Splendid in its isolation on a
floodplain north of Kaza, Ki Gompa
is Spiti's largest Buddhist monastery

09

An attractive Portuguese colonial settlement by the sea, Salvador in Bahia is Brazil's third most populous city with almost 3 million inhabitants

TOP 10 REGIONS

BAHIA, BRAZIL

Bahia has always had a certain wow factor. Located on the northeast coast of Brazil, it's a tropical paradise of white sandy beaches and clear blue water, islands surrounded by coral reefs, plantations rich with cocoa beans, and Parque Nacional da Chapada Diamantina, famous for its wild waterfalls. But Bahia's natural playground is suddenly more accessible to tourists, thanks to the facelift that Salvador – a Portuguese colonial city that's also the state capital – underwent after being chosen as a host city for the 2014 FIFA World Cup. There's never been a better time, or an easier time, to explore the birthplace of Afro-Brazilian culture.

Population: 15.2 million
Main town: Salvador
Language: Portuguese
Unit of currency: Real
How to get there:
Most travellers
arrive in Bahia via the
international airport in
Salvador, but it's also
possible to book flights
into the smaller airports
in Ilhéus or Porto
Seguro. Most coastal
destinations are well
connected by bus.

Capoeira, Trancoso.
Salvador de Bahia, Brazil

MELBA PHOTO AGENCY © ALAMY STOCK PHOTO

TELL ME MORE...

Brazilians have a nickname for Bahia: '*Terra da Felicidade*' (Land of Happiness). It makes sense. There's the sunshine-drenched climate, for starters, and water that's warm enough to swim in year-round. And there's a distinctive local character found nowhere else in the world, born out of a centuries-old cultural collision of colonial Portuguese settlers, native Brazilians and Africans brought to Salvador during the slave trade. The result is a fascinating medley of architectural styles, culinary customs and artistic traditions, not to mention a collective inclination to throw a good party. Bahia is ground zero for some of the liveliest festivals in a country that's famous for them, whether

'Afro-Brazilian culture is particularly present in Salvador. Capoeira and Candomblé are the main expressions – powerful, popular and rich. And you cannot experience them truly, in all their magnitude, other than here.'
Jaqueline Oliveira, choreographer, painter, activist and Salvador resident

ITINERARY
Two weeks in Bahia

Start off in Bahia's charming bay-front capital **Salvador** for a quick introduction to Afro-Brazilian culture and cuisine.

Take a two-hour boat ride from Salvador to the idyllic tropical island **Morro de São Paulo** and its quieter sister, Ilha de Boipeba.

Get off the beaten path – and to some of the best beaches in Brazil – at **Península de Maraú**.

Surf's up at the popular enclave of **Itacaré**, a good base for exploring the beaches of Bahia's Cocoa Coast.

Seek out **Arraial d'Ajuda**, a gorgeous beach getaway within easy distance of sleepy Trancoso and party-centric Porto Seguro.

they're celebrating Carnaval, paying tribute to a patron saint on his feast day, or honouring an *orisha* (deity) in a Candomblé ceremony. Bahians are characterised by joie de vivre. Luckily for travellers, locals are inclusive: everyone is welcome to join the dancing in the street or the party on the beach.

UNMISSABLE EXPERIENCES

• Sample *moqueca*, a classic Bahian seafood stew made with fresh shellfish, coconut milk, tomatoes, onion, and *dendê oil*, an African palm oil now produced in the region. Pair with a caipirinha, the national cocktail.

• Catch a performance of capoeira, a Bahian art form that fuses dance and martial arts. Capoeira was invented by African slaves as a discreet way of practising self-defence without attracting the attention of their captors. Today, you can see modern capoeiristas' graceful athleticism at performances in public squares, or by stepping into a capoeira school in the Pelourinho, the historic centre of Salvador.

TIME YOUR VISIT

Carnaval is the event of the year in Bahia, with the biggest celebrations happening in Salvador. In 2018, the party kicks off on 8 February and ends on 13 February. It's a lively time to visit, but plan ahead: prices sky-rocket and many *pousadas* (guesthouses) are booked out months in advance.

• By Bridget Gleeson

1 Salvador
Morro de São Paulo 2
3 Península de Maraú
4 Itacaré
5 Arraial d'Ajuda

People walk in Pelourinho area, famous Historic Centre of Salvador, Bahia in Brazil

LOS HAITISES
NATIONAL PARK, DOMINICAN REPUBLIC

In the south of Samaná Bay, Parque Nacional Los Haitises is a 1375-sq-km patchwork of craggy islets, blue canals and verdant forest, an ecosystem that appears plucked from prehistory. Venture deep into the park and you'll find yourself in the heart of the Dominican Republic's cultural history. Los Haitises is hardly a well-kept secret, but visitor numbers are rising: some big hotel projects are brewing nearby, so get here before the crowds arrive. An updated sustainability plan will enhance park infrastructure and preservation, so you'll be greeted with improved trails and facilities.

A verdant jewel in the north of the Dominican Republic, Los Haitises became a National Park in 1976

10

Population: 110 bird species, 700 plant species
Main town: Accessed from Sabana de la Mar and Las Terrenas
Language: Spanish
Unit of currency: Dominican peso
How to get there: Most visitors will fly into the Dominican Republic's main airport (located just east of Santo Domingo) and reach the national park either from Sabana de la Mar or via boat tours from the Samaná Peninsula. However, some flights connect to El Catey International Airport, located between Nagua and Sánchez.

TELL ME MORE...

Seen from the open waters of Samaná Bay, Los Haitises National Park is a range of vivid green hills punctuating the shoreline; 'los haitises' means 'highlands' in the Taíno language. As you enter Los Haitises' maze, you'll feel like an explorer in uncharted territory; the only sounds will be your boat gliding over water and numerous winged companions flying overhead.

Perhaps the most unique feature of Los Haitises is the series of limestone caves worn ragged with water erosion and streaked with salt. Pass into the yawning 'Boca del Tiburón' (Shark's Mouth) before swinging around to shore to explore caves that were once ceremonial grounds for the Taíno people; these caves – La Cueva de San Gabriel and Las Cuevas de la Arena, among others – contain well-preserved carvings and paintings depicting animals, deities, medicine men and even the Spanish cross.

UNMISSABLE EXPERIENCES

• Take a motorised boat tour to zip through larger waterways and take in pristine views. For

ITINERARY
Five days around Los Haitises

Sip mojitos at **El Mosquito**, the coolest new bar in hip Las Terrenas.

Ride on horseback to **Cascada El Limón**, one of the most picturesque waterfalls in the Dominican Republic.

Hop over to Las Galeras to enjoy **Playa Rincón**, one of the northern DR's best beaches.

Catch a ride from Samaná town to the jewel-like island of **Cayo Levantado**, and lounge on its sparkling public beach.

Spend the day cruising cerulean channels and taking in the unique scenery of **Los Haitises National Park**.

a more relaxed approach, embark on a kayaking tour through smaller inlets and mangrove forests, or drift in the open waters at sunrise to catch the best views of abundant bird life.

• Check in at the impressive eco-lodge Paraíso Caño Hondo, located west of Sabana de la Mar. It's a good base for exploring and offers several guided tours. Bonus: the Río Jivales passes through the property, forming several pools to enjoy after a long day adventuring.

TIME YOUR VISIT

Precipitation falls heavily in the rainy season. The best timing for sunny skies is from December to April, when the region is driest. The good weather window comes with a bonus: humpback whales visit Samaná from January to late March, so you just might see a friendly sea giant or two.

• By Bailey Freeman

'It has a unique landscape where we find an immense and rich natural diversity: caves, mountains, mangroves, lagoons and unique species. It's truly a wonder on Earth.' *Silvia Clerici, local tour operator*

Pelicans share the park with parrots, owls, magnificent frigatebirds and numerous other feathered species

LONELY PLANET'S

TOP 10
CITIES

Seville, Spain / Detroit, USA / Canberra, Australia / Hamburg, Germany
Kaohsiung, Taiwan / Antwerp, Belgium / Matera, Italy / San Juan, Puerto Rico
Guanajuato, Mexico / Oslo, Norway

01

Looking out across
the Old Town in Seville,
Andalucía's exhilarating capital

TOP 10 CITIES

SEVILLE, SPAIN

Over the past 10 years, Seville has transformed itself. Once a traffic-congested metropolis resting on its historical laurels, Seville has bloomed into a city of bicycles and trams, keen to reinvigorate its artistic past. The metamorphosis hasn't gone unnoticed. The capital of Andalucía will host the 31st European Film Awards in 2018, and showcases its good looks in the TV fantasy drama *Game of Thrones*. Adding colour to an ongoing artistic renaissance, Seville is in the midst of celebrating the 400th anniversary of homegrown Baroque painter Bartolomé Esteban Murillo, with half a dozen one-of-a-kind expositions continuing into 2018.

Population: 690,000
Language: Spanish
Unit of currency: Euro
How to get there: Seville's international airport, located 10km from the city centre, has daily flights to various European cities including London, Paris, Frankfurt and Amsterdam. Alternatively, high-speed AVE trains travel regularly to Madrid (2½ hours).

TELL ME MORE...

Seville is a city of atmosphere as much as sights. Amid the aromatic orange trees and poignant public processions, the mood is ever-changing, from the solemnity of Semana Santa (Holy Week) to the merriment of the spring Feria, a huge six-day fair. Whether sombre or joyous, life here is always lived passionately. Flamenco

'I love Seville because of the atmosphere in the streets. There are always people hanging out in the squares, streets and bars. To experience it, I recommend visiting the Plaza del Salvador.'
Pedro Arriola, CEO, Pancho Tours

artists treat every performance as if it's their last, operas depict hot-blooded heroines and unscrupulous Figaros, while bars and restaurants manage to capture the latest food and fashion trends while standing by their age-old traditions – jolly good tapas.

All around the city's neighbourhoods, tradition spars with innovation. The results are rarely mundane. In the central district all roads lead to one of the world's largest cathedrals, a Gothic anchor to Seville's medieval Santa

ITINERARY
Two days in Seville

- One of the largest Christian churches in the world, Seville's **Cathedral** has a glorious Moorish bell-tower and a rich cache of 'golden century' art.

- **Alcázar**, a Moorish-influenced castle complex long inhabited by Christian kings, is redolent of Granada's Alhambra with its colonnaded patios and lush gardens.

- Seville has dozens of places to see genre-defining art, but the epoch-transcending **Museo de Bellas Artes**, in an old convent, collates the best work.

- Opened to the public for the first time in 2016, the **Palacio de las Dueñas** (home of the late Duchess of Alba) is a museum of all things Sevillano.

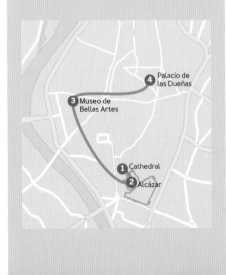

Cruz quarter. Not far away, futuristic visions materialise at the multi-functional Metropol Parasol, a huge canopy of latticed wood held up by five mushroom-like pillars.

UNMISSABLE EXPERIENCES

• Flamenco is Andalucía's quintessential performance art. This amalgamation of song, guitar and dance is partly rooted in Seville and the city puts on high-quality, authentic shows every night of the week. Choose between rambunctious bars, private flamenco clubs or large auditoriums offering more choreographed dinner shows.

• Seville has developed some of Spain's most innovative tapas bars, but it also safeguards classics such as El Rinconcillo, a restaurant that purports to be the oldest in Spain (founded in 1670). For high-octane tapas bar strips with fusion food, head to Calle Betis in Triana, or the Alameda de Hércules.

TIME YOUR VISIT

Spring is the obvious time to visit. Seville hosts two of the biggest festivals in Spain (Semana Santa and Feria de Abril), both moveable feasts depending on when Easter falls. The heat of high summer is best avoided. For cooler temperatures and cheaper prices, arrive in September or October.

• By Brendan Sainsbury

Seville provides seemingly limitless opportunities for dining al fresco into the night

The semicircular, colonnaded Plaza de Espana
has appeared in several films including *Star
Wars* and *Lawrence of Arabia*

DETROIT, USA

After decades of neglect, Detroit is rolling again. It's like the whole place is caffeine-buzzed, freewheeling in ideas. Young creative types jump-started the scene when they began transforming the crazy-huge slew of abandoned buildings into distilleries, bike shops and galleries. This sparked fresh public works, such as the just-opened hockey and basketball arena downtown, and the QLine streetcar that gives easy access to city hot spots. More are coming: three new parks will extend the riverfront trail (ideal for two-wheeling via the new 43-station bike-share scheme in the greater downtown area), plus groovy hotels will emerge from an old wig shop and a forlorn parking lot.

REESE LASSMAN / EYEEM © GETTY IMAGES

The Art Deco skyscrapers of
downtown Detroit, a city that is
bouncing back after years of decline

02

Population: 677,000
(4.3 million across metropolitan area)

Language: English

Unit of currency: US dollar

How to get there: Detroit Metropolitan Airport is one of the USA's largest airports and a regional hub, with many domestic and international flights. Amtrak trains also chug into town.

TELL ME MORE...

Nowhere else looks like Detroit. Massive art deco skyscrapers cluster downtown, relics from the city's wealthy, car-making heyday. Then the place fell apart: industry declined and 60% of the population has bolted since the 1960s, leaving behind eerie ruins and emptiness, like a post-apocalyptic movie set. Experiencing this tumbledown landscape is part of the Detroit package.

Now the city is clawing its way back, and the can-

do energy is palpable. Take the innovators who bought a beat-up auto dealership, hung provocative art in the raw space, and launched MOCAD (the Museum of Contemporary Art Detroit). Or the organisers of Slow Roll, who gathered a few friends for a bicycle ride that has morphed into 4000 hipsters, urban teens

PEETER VIISIMAA © GETTY IMAGES

A mural in the thriving retail district of Eastern Market says it all

'Detroit is full of dreamers and people who value community. Creativity and innovation are more highly valued here than money or status.'
Mark Wallace, resident and CEO of Detroit RiverFront Conservancy

ITINERARY
Two days in Detroit

- Take the QLine to **Midtown** for art-museum gawking, Jack White's record shop, and cool-cat cafes and breweries.
- Hop on a bicycle and pedal along the **RiverWalk** from downtown's hulking skyscrapers to pretty Belle Isle, where kayaking, walking trails and a glass-domed conservatory await.
- Browse **Eastern Market** for produce and crafts on the weekends, and eye-popping murals any day. Bonus for cyclists: the graffiti-splashed Dequindre Cut Greenway zips here from the riverfront.
- Loosen the belt for **Corktown,** Detroit's buzziest 'hood. Chow pickle-brined fried chicken at Gold Cash Gold, then hit Two James Spirits for a tonic in the distillery's tasting room.

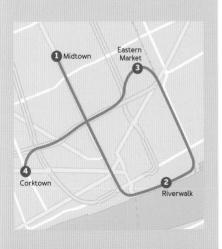

and suburban families pedalling together on a community jaunt each week. Meanwhile, murals keep brightening derelict buildings, urban farms keep sprouting in vacant lots, and chefs keep cooking in inventive restaurants. Scrappiness rules in this gritty city.

UNMISSABLE EXPERIENCES
- Step into the sky-lit hall at the Detroit Institute of Arts where Diego Rivera's *Detroit Industry* surrounds you on 27 panels. He's the city's original muralist, and his whopping work tells Detroit's blue-collar labour history in vivid colour. Beyond are troves of Picassos, suits of armour and modern African-American paintings.
- A visit to The Henry Ford Museum, which holds the industrialist's stash of Americana, lets you walk through history: past the chair Lincoln was sitting in when he was assassinated, into the bus on which Rosa Parks refused to give up her seat, and lots more. It's in suburban Dearborn, next to Detroit.

TIME YOUR VISIT
Detroit has cold winters, and many outdoor activities shut down for the season. Better to visit when the weather mellows. The popular Slow Roll bike rides happen on Mondays from May to October. Movement Electronic Music Festival, one of the world's largest of its kind, takes place the last weekend in May.
- By Karla Zimmerman

03

Canberra's National Museum
of Australia sits on the shore
of Lake Burley Griffin

TOP 10 CITIES

CANBERRA, AUSTRALIA

Criminally overlooked Canberra packs a big punch for such a small city. National treasures are found round almost every corner and exciting new boutique precincts have emerged, bulging with gastronomic highlights and cultural must-dos. This is the first year that Canberra's picturesque Manuka Oval will host an International Test cricket match, providing sporting fans the perfect excuse to visit Australia's federal capital. Later in 2018 the Australian War Memorial will take centre stage as it hosts the 100th anniversary of the WWI Armistice; a series of commemorative events will take place on 11 November 2018.

Population: 390,000

Language: English

Unit of currency: Australian dollar

How to get there: Fly directly into Canberra via Singapore or hop on one of the many domestic connections from most of Australia's state capitals. Alternatively, driving from Sydney takes a little over three hours.

TELL ME MORE...

Visiting Canberra unlocks the Australian psyche. Admire an extraordinary volume of treasures in the Australian National Gallery, National Library and Australian War Memorial. Beyond these stately monuments and galleries, the 250-hectare National Arboretum is home to a whopping 94 forests of rare, endangered and symbolic Australian fauna criss-crossed with walking and cycling trails. The Arboretum also features one of Australia's quirkiest playgrounds, with massive acorns on stilts and play areas shaped like banksia pods.

Revitalised precincts such as NewActon and Braddon best illustrate Canberra's new lease of life. The deliciously decorated Hotel Hotel in NewActon is the epitome of new Canberra style, with materials such as reclaimed wood evoking the Australian landscape. NewActon is also home to A Baker, where the five-course 'Just Feed Me' and 'Just Wine Me' selections offer a perfect array of locally sourced produce and wine. Meanwhile, a brilliant blend of pop-up shops and lively cafes are sprinkled along Lonsdale Street in boutique Braddon.

ITINERARY
Three days in Canberra

• Trot off to breakfast at **The Cupping Room,** which serves coffee from Canberra's largest speciality coffee roaster.

• Hire a bike and pedal across to **Parkes,** enjoying views of Lake Burley Griffin along the way, before getting a culture fix of national galleries and museums.

• Stop at the **Canberra Glassworks** where you can watch contemporary glass art being shaped before your eyes.

• Get political and see the suits in action at **Parliament House** (open daily).

• Book an excursion with **Canberra Winery Tours** to visit award-winning Lerida Estate, or find out about small batch bottling at down-to-earth Murrumbateman Winery.

03

'Canberra is the best of city and country. We get all the perks of being near the bush, an impressive food and wine scene, and an experimental art scene. There are always things going on... especially if you dig.' *Nicole Short, general manager, Hotel Hotel*

Poppies at the Australian War Memorial, which was originally commissioned to honour the fallen of WWI and opened in 1941

RICHARD GUNN © GETTY IMAGES

UNMISSABLE EXPERIENCES

• A shrine, museum and archive, the Australian War Memorial was established as a place to pay homage to Australians who lost their lives in conflict. This memorial is a beautiful and humbling place to celebrate – and reflect upon – life and loss.

• Works from the world's largest collection of Aboriginal and Torres Strait Islander art (over 7500 pieces) are on display at the National Gallery of Australia (NGA). Also home to Sidney Nolan's Ned Kelly series, the NGA's depth of Australian works is the perfect historical storyboard of the turbulence and triumphs of this island continent.

TIME YOUR VISIT

Canberra explodes in colour from mid-September to mid-October when it plays host to Floriade, an annual festival of a million blooms. Floriade has blossomed into a month-long festival of music, cultural celebrations, horticultural workshops and markets. Another great time to visit is from March to May, when the city glows with autumnal colours.

• By Chris Zeiher

TOP 10 CITIES

HAMBURG, GERMANY

Its completion seemed to take longer than sitting through the entire cycle of Wagner's *Ring* operas, but the stunning new €790 million Elbphilharmonie concert hall was worth every extra year of delay. The glass top shimmers like crystalline sails while the base reflects the brick aesthetic of the surrounding historic and oh-so-walkable HafenCity port area. From here, alluringly accessible Hamburg radiates out along its vast harbour and the Elbe River. Surprises abound: three-season riverfront beach bars, nightlife that's among Europe's best, and low-rise charms that reward wanderers who use the city's dozens of old steeples as compass points.

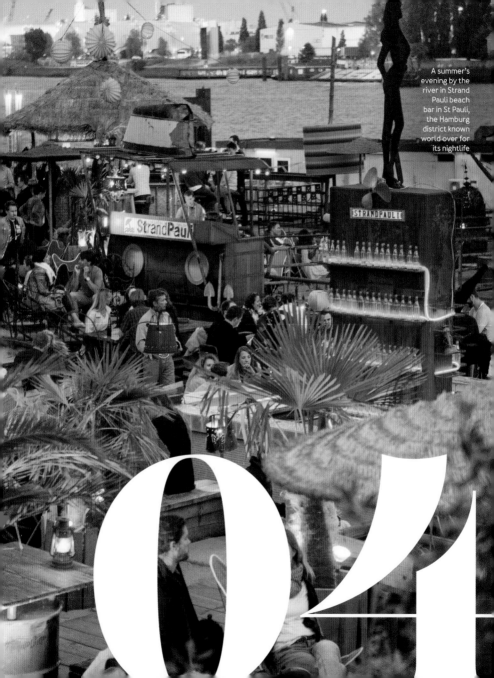

A summer's evening by the river in Strand Pauli beach bar in St Pauli, the Hamburg district known world over for its nightlife

04

Population: 1.7 million

Language: German

Unit of currency: Euro

How to get there: Hamburg's international airport receives flights from around Europe and a few from North America. It has excellent rail connections from across Germany and neighbouring countries.

TELL ME MORE...

The second-largest city in Germany, Hamburg throbs with international beats (especially in its legendary clubs). At times you'll forget you're even in Deutschland, thanks to the city's unique stew of different cultures. Walk down a pedestrian street and you'll pass a Portuguese

'Hamburg is like a diamond showing many facets: old parks, the river, world heritage, the Elbphilharmonie and last – but not least – its people: a great mix living peacefully together.'
Anja Frauböse, corporate communications manager, Hamburg resident

seafood bistro, a Middle Eastern market and a designer boutique that defies categorisation. This openness to outside influences dates back over the centuries since Hamburg became a prominent trading city in the Hanseatic League in the 1200s. The city has lived for its maritime links to the outside world ever since, a legacy recognised by Unesco in 2015.

In Hamburg there's always a sense of closeness to the water. Even when you think you're inland, you'll spot an impossibly large freighter gliding through breaks in the waterfront. And if you're in the somewhat

ITINERARY
A long weekend in Hamburg

- Head to **Elbphilharmonie** to see a show, have a drink, marvel at the architecture or go up high for city views.

- Experience **Miniatur Wunderland** – even cynics are jaw-dropped converts after they thrill to hundreds of model trains weaving through carefully replicated landscapes.

- Sip your way around **Strandperle** to enjoy the best of Hamburg's riverfront beach bars.

- Crane your neck as you admire **Mahnmal St Nikolai**, a towering steeple with bitter WWII history.

- Hurl yourself into **St Georg**'s unmissable mix of restaurants and nightlife. Elbow in with the effervescent crowd at Bar M&V, the perfect venue to begin – or end – your night.

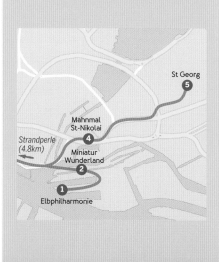

seedy Reeperbahn red-light district, where The Beatles found their groove in the early 1960s, you'll hear the cry of gulls overhead.

UNMISSABLE EXPERIENCES

• Don't miss one of Hamburg's many port tours. Take the U3 U-Bahn subway line, which rattles above ground with stunning city views, to the central Landungsbrücken and pick your boat. Opt for one of the longer tours, so you can savour the best of Hamburg's watery sights and sounds – like crashing, banging containers whizzing on and off huge ships – while relaxing on deck with a beer.

• Early on Sunday, thousands of locals and visitors (many straight from the clubs) hit the famous Fischmarkt in St Pauli. Drink beer, buy fish and listen to live German pop music.

TIME YOUR VISIT

When to visit Hamburg is as easy as knowing the seasons. In winter there are convivial Christmas markets, where you can sup mulled wine while mulling over gifts. Spring and autumn witness outdoor life that defies blustery days, while the city lives outside during the long summer days.

• By Ryan Ver Berkmoes

The striking facade of the Elbphilharmonie lurks behind the warehouses and merchant quarters of the harbour district

LENA SERDITOVA © SHUTTERSTOCK

Most pagodas and temples around Kaohsiung's Lotus Pond were built in the 20th-century, including the 1953 Spring and Autumn Pavilions

05

KAOHSIUNG, TAIWAN

A massive arts centre and 100,000 sq m music complex, complete with banyan-caressed plazas and wave-lapped walkways, is emerging on Kaohsiung's balmy harbourfront – Taiwan's showcase for experimental architecture from around the world. Adding to this will be a spectacular cruise terminal, for those favouring an Odyssean approach to the port city. A sleek 36-station light-rail system links these monuments to the rest of Kaohsiung. Further inland, on the Xiaogang Shan trail, hikers can view the Taiwan Strait from a new 27m skywalk, a reminder that water is ever-present. Kaohsiung is surging with possibilities: visit before the world gets wind of it.

'Dome of Light', in the unlikely setting of Formosa Boulevard metro station, is claimed to be the world's largest glass artwork

Population: 2.8 million
Languages: Mandarin, Taiwanese
Unit of currency: New Taiwan dollar
How to get there: Kaohsiung International Airport, aka Xiaogang Airport, has flights to most Southeast Asian countries, Japan, Korea and China. Located south of the city, it connects seamlessly to downtown by metro.

TELL ME MORE...

Taiwan's second-largest city is a hub of industry. It's also a modern landscape of wide streets, airy cafes, sultry jazz dens and riverside parks. Beaches skirt the urban area, 1000 hectares of forest bristle on its doorstep, and Cijin fishing village is but a ferry-bob away. Like the rest of

Taiwan, the city teems with temples, ranging from fun, shrill-coloured kitsch to elegant edifices by masters of folk art.

Futuristic cultural spaces are sprouting, their designs commissioned through worldwide architectural competitions. Kaohsiung is where southern traditions enjoy a 21st-century spin, where acrylic meets rust and ship-wood in galleries, and chefs reimagine heirloom recipes for the modern palate. Want more? It's home to a robust LGBT scene, contemporary indigenous art, and the largest organic farmers' market in southern Taiwan. And wherever you go, whether by

05
BEST IN
TRAVEL
2O18

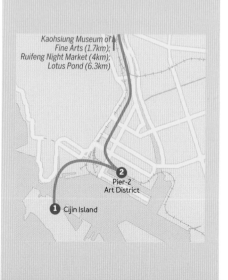

---

metro or the city's burgeoning fleet of public bikes, Kaohsiung greets with a laid-back maritime charm.

ITINERARY
Three days in Kaohsiung

• Take a 10-minute ferry ride to **Cijin Island** for the beautiful Tianhou Temple, fresh seafood and a coastal park.

• Browse **Pier-2 Art District**'s galleries, boutiques and cafes. It's best to visit after 2pm.

• Contemporary indigenous art and art from southern Taiwan are the highlights of the laudable **Kaohsiung Museum of Fine Arts**.

• **Ruifeng Night Market**, Kaohsiung's largest, is where peckish locals go for braised pig's ear and fruity concoctions.

• Picturesque **Lotus Pond** is fringed by two dozen pagodas and pavilions – some evoking 1960s pop-art kitsch, some subdued and serene, such as the Confucius Temple.

UNMISSABLE EXPERIENCES

• Along two sweeping boulevards by a stark blue harbour, banana and bicycle warehouses from the 1970s shelter Pier-2 Art District, an array of galleries, boutiques, cafes and entertainment spots. It's a lovely place to linger for at least half a day. A flea market spreads its wares here on weekend afternoons.

• Far-flung Stone Temple is an interpretation of a Chinese Taoist temple by Southeast Asian migrant workers who created it with seashells, coral, stones and bucket-loads of imagination. Taoist deities stand guard along wavy colonnaded corridors. It's like nothing you've ever seen, though 'Gaudí-esque' comes to mind.

'I enjoy drinking with pals at the seafood restaurants. Kaohsiung is the distribution point for seafood from all of southern Taiwan, so imagine the variety and freshness! Best with beer or whisky!'
Trista Liao, guesthouse owner

TIME YOUR VISIT

You can visit Kaohsiung all year round, though the best times are October to March or April, when it's cooler. Kaohsiung has a tropical climate and temperatures soar to over 30°C from June to September, which is great for swimming. Monsoon season is June to October.

• By Piera Chen

Kaohsiung Museum of Fine Arts (1.7km);
Ruifeng Night Market (4km);
Lotus Pond (6.3km)

2 Pier-2 Art District

1 Cijin Island

The 1976 seven-storey Dragon and Tiger pagodas at Lotus Pond belong to the Chiji Palace temple to which they are connected by a walkway

TOP 10 CITIES

ANTWERP, BELGIUM

Once northern Europe's greatest city, today Antwerp is one of its best-kept secrets. Flanders' unofficial capital is laden with historic riches and home to world-class arts and design, and this year it's showing its cultural chops with a celebration of its Baroque heyday. Inspired by the city's most famous resident, Rubens, Antwerp Baroque 2018 will feature Flemish Masters rubbing shoulders with modern talent in a calendar that spans parades, concerts, street art, multimedia shows and workshops. Not that Antwerp's residents need an excuse to unleash their creativity: the city, especially its former docks, is flush with pop-up bars, farm-to-fork joints and architectural showstoppers.

REPISTU © GETTY IMAGES

Antwerp is unafraid to showcase modernity among all that Baroque – the cutting-edge Museum aan de Stroom opened its doors in 2011

06

Population: 510,000
Languages: Dutch, English
Unit of currency: Euro

How to get there: Antwerp is 30 minutes by train from Brussels, just over an hour from Amsterdam, and two hours from Paris; its beautiful fin-de-siècle station is almost worth the trip in itself. A small airport also hosts flights from London and several locations in Spain.

TELL ME MORE...

Antwerp pairs Bruges-style good looks with big-city cool. In its old town, grand, gingerbread-house facades and cobbled lanes are overlooked by a soaring Gothic cathedral – the Low Countries' tallest. Golden Age glory abounds in museums stuffed with works by Flemish Masters – and the creative scene,

fuelled by world-renowned art and fashion schools, remains red hot. You'll find inventive spirit in countless galleries and a staggering array of boutiques, design shops and vintage hoards offering up everything from Dries Van Noten designer dresses to three-euro threads.

Though Antwerp doesn't skimp on Belgian classics such as beer, chocolate and the gin-like *genever*, the port city is unafraid to push the boat out when it comes to food and drink, especially in the old docklands of Het Eilandje. Currently reviving at a rate of knots, its warehouses brim with coffee shops, cocktail bars and restaurants, mingling with hi-tech museums and futuristic creations by the likes of Zaha Hadid.

The showpiece of the city's market square, the Rennaisance-style Stadhuis, completed in 1565, is fronted by the Brabo Fountain

© WWW.WOODMONKEY.BE / VISITANTWERPEN.BE

BEST IN
TRAVEL
2o18

'Antwerp is a cosmopolitan city that fits in your pocket. You can find world-class architecture, design and cuisine and still bump into a friend walking to a gig on a Friday night.'

Jona De Beuckeleer, co-founder and guide, Cyclant bike tours and hire

UNMISSABLE EXPERIENCES

• Antwerp's house-museums heave with Golden Age treasures. In the Unesco-listed Museum Plantin-Moretus, the creaking, timbered home of a printing pioneer, you'll find ceiling-high stacks of inky type and the world's oldest presses, plus rare books and maps. The Rubenshuis, the artist's restored home and studio, is crammed with rare art.

• Compact but contrasting, Antwerp is a great place to hit the saddle. A bike ride of a few hours is enough to explore the old town and docklands, street art-filled Park Spoor Noord, Art-Nouveau Zurenborg and Antwerp's left bank with its postcard-worthy skyline.

TIME YOUR VISIT

Antwerp Baroque 2018's festivities are liveliest from March to September; spring and early summer are especially good times for big-ticket events. High summer brings numerous festivals, from Museumnacht, with its late openings and all-night party, to indie, jazz and electronic music blowouts including Summerfestival, Jazz Middelheim and Tomorrowland.

• By Sophie McGrath

ITINERARY
A long weekend in Antwerp

• Gaze at soaring columns and Rubens altarpieces in the **Cathedral of Our Lady,** a medieval masterpiece that was nearly two centuries in the making.

• Gorge on **The Chocolate Line**'s experimental creations, like bacon, tequila and wasabi chocs, 'pills' for the lovesick and snortable cocoa.

• Treasure-hunt along **Kloosterstraat,** whose boutiques, concept shops and antiques emporiums sell everything from statement fashion to Soviet maps.

• Swig a *bolleke* glass of Antwerp beer at the storied – and recently refurbished – **De Koninck brewery,** with food pairings from artisan producers.

• Visit Het Eilandje's high-design **MAS** museum for immersive exhibits and panoramic views.

Built (though still not completed) between 1352 and 1521, the Cathedral of Our Lady has dominated the Antwerp skyline for 500 years

MARIOGUTI © GETTY IMAGES

07

Tumbledown tunnels, alleyways and stone dwellings climb the hillsides of Matera in Italy's Basilicata region

MATERA, ITALY

██████ **A crown of honey-stoned houses** perched above a ravine, Matera has knockout looks. But that's only half the story: snaking beneath the surface is a labyrinth of cave dwellings, churches and monasteries that date back over 9000 years – making it one of the oldest living cities in the world. Largely restored from near-ruin, Matera's now capitalising on its cavernous appeal, with hotels, restaurants and bars carving out a scene as cool as their rock-hewn walls. There's a flurry of events planned ahead of its stint as a European Capital of Culture for 2019, so visit now before this underground destination emerges into the limelight.

Population: 60,500
Language: Italian
Unit of currency: Euro
How to get there: Matera is 90 minutes by bus or train
from Bari airport, which receives flights from around
Italy and Europe. It's also just over four hours by bus
from Naples and six hours from Rome.

TELL ME MORE...

Think Florence and Rome have history?
They're young guns compared to Matera,
whose cliff-side caves have been occupied
and expanded by peasants, monks and artisans
since prehistoric times. Located in a remote
part of Basilicata, the long-overlooked 'arch'
of Italy's boot, the Unesco-listed site feels
bypassed by time – it's no surprise it's twinned
with fellow hidden city Petra. An Escher-like
maze that often doubles for biblical towns in
movies, its alleyways, tunnels and staircases
twist between thousands of caves, many bearing
traces of the past, from Paleolithic grottoes
and *palazzo* ruins to the crowning glory of 155
Byzantine churches, many lined with frescoes.

But the *Città Sotterranea* (Underground
City) is no museum: though forcibly emptied in
the 1950s amid headline-making poverty, today
it houses a growing community that's proudly
bringing its past out of the shadows, and
injecting new life with ventures from minimalist
suites and restaurants serving local *cucina
povera* to festivals and multimedia exhibits.

ITINERARY
Two days in Matera

- Glimpse how Matera's cave-dwellers
(and their animals) once lived in the recreated
rooms of the **Casa Grotta di Vico Solitario.**
- Hike into the **gorge** east of Matera,
exploring its grottoes and cave churches
before ascending to a belvedere with
cinematic city views.
- Back in town, traverse the vast, vaulted
chambers of the 16th-century **Palombaro
Lungo,** one of the world's largest cisterns.
- Join locals for a *passeggiata* (evening stroll)
in the **Piazza Vittoria Veneto,** a lively square.
- Dig into specialities such as *lucanica* sausage
and *cacioricotta* cheese at **Baccanti,** before
slurping on lavender or fig gelato at **I Vizi
degli Angeli.**

The subterranean *sassi* (cave districts) of Matera were first inhabited in Paleolithic times

LIANEM © GETTY IMAGES

07

BEST IN TRAVEL 2018

UNMISSABLE EXPERIENCES

Exploring Matera's *sassi* (cave districts) is the highlight of any visit – strike out alone or with a guide from an operator such as SassiWeb or Viator. Don't miss the Chiesa di Madonna delle Virtù, a millennia-old monastic complex spread over two storeys and countless caves, adjoined by a vividly frescoed church. Find contemporary art at MUSMA, a gallery focused on sculpture that is itself sequestered amid the deep caves and frescoed rooms of a historic *palazzo*. It's also the place to book a visit to the Cripta del Peccato Originale outside town, known as the Sistine Chapel of cave churches for its rich frescoes.

'People are kind, flavours authentic and, even on the busiest day, in minutes I can be in the *sassi* and lost in another world.'
Mikaela Bandini, owner of Area 8 cafe and bar

TIME YOUR VISIT

July and August are peak months for holidays and festivities alike – from the Procession of Shepherds, a parade of papier-mâché floats with a grand ripping-apart, to Gezziamoci, bringing jazz to the caves and the plateau beyond. Dodge the heat of a southern Italian summer by visiting in spring or early autumn.

• By Sophie McGrath

SAN JUAN, PUERTO RÍCO

San Juan is coming into its own, a place where old meets new, where the city's colonial past meshes comfortably with an emerging modern urbanity. Old San Juan is a walled enclave with cobblestoned roads, leafy plazas, and historic churches and forts. Beyond the walls, modern San Juan is draped with murals, and its cadre of museums and galleries form a dynamic art scene. New, innovative restaurants are opening, with many farm-to-table eateries beckoning foodies and casual diners alike. The exuberant nightlife – dance clubs, lounges, bars, casinos – has long been a highlight, while San Juan's beaches remain as dazzling as ever.

Old San Juan's leafy colonial-era cobblestoned streets are a delight to wander

08

Population: 355,000

Languages: Spanish, English

Unit of currency: US dollar

How to get there: Luis Muñoz Marín International Airport, located 12km east of Old San Juan, is the main entry point to the city from mainland USA and beyond. A second airport in the middle of town, Isla Grande, is a one-room affair serving nearby islands.

TELL ME MORE...

San Juan has many faces, from laid-back Caribbean to modern hipster. Old San Juan transports you to times gone by. Colonial-era buildings, men playing dominoes and couples strolling plazas are all scenes reminiscent of life lived more slowly, before screens and status updates. But look closely and you'll also find fresh energy: lounge bars and salsa clubs buzzing with young San Juaneros, local coffee shops packed with young professionals, and restaurants playing with flavours and fusion cuisine.

Neighbourhoods such as Santurce and Ocean Park are known for their arty vibe, with murals – some 10 storeys high – emblazoned on building walls.

San Juan's affluent Condado district draws visitors to its sandy beach and waterside hotels

DENNIS K. JOHNSON © GETTY IMAGES

'I love Antojitos del Callejon. The salsa music, the dancing, the food – their alcapurrillas (plantain-based fritters) are so good! The ocean is right there too. To me, it's everything San Juan.' *Lalo Ramírez, San Juanero*

ITINERARY
A weekend in San Juan

- A Unesco World Heritage Site, the magnificent fort **El Morro** provides an insight into life in colonial times.
- While exploring Old San Juan, stop for a cup of Puerto Rican coffee at cosy cafe **Finca Cialitos.**
- Enjoy centuries of Puerto Rican art at the celebrated **Museo de Arte de Puerto Rico.**
- **La Placita de Santurce** comes alive on weekend evenings for live music, bar-hopping, and some of the city's best restaurants.
- A beach backed by high-rise condos, gorgeous **Playa Isla Verde** has soft sand, towering palms and calm waters.

Finca Cialitos (3km);
El Morro (4km)

Museo de Arte
de Puerto Rico
④
La Placita
de Santurce ③

Playa Isla
Verde (2.8km)

Here, food trucks and farm-to-table eateries are popping up everywhere. Nearby, Condado neighbourhood is upscale with a thriving LGBT scene: rainbow flags, boutique shops, high-end hotels and sleek casinos are the norm. And, oh, the beaches! From Isla Verde to Puerta de Tierra are shimmering ribbons of sand, swaying palms and mellow surf.

UNMISSABLE EXPERIENCES
Old San Juan is the city's colonial and historic heart, a favourite among locals and a must-see for visitors. Simply wandering around is a delight: blue-toned cobblestoned streets pass verdant plazas and centuries-old buildings painted in pastel colours. All paths eventually lead to Plaza de Armas, the old city's main plaza, with live *bomba* drumming on many weekend evenings. Old San Juan is also home to some of the city's best museums and sights: Museo de las Américas traces the cultural history of the Americas, while the colonial-era fort El Morro has breathtaking views of the ocean from atop huge stone walls.

TIME YOUR VISIT
Head to San Juan between December and May, when blue skies and balmy weather rule. It's also a time of vibrant festivals – from the week-long Fiestas de la Calle San Sebastián in January to the popular Puerto Rico JazzFest in March – so you might find it tough to leave...

• By Liza Prado

09

The Bell Tower of the Basilica de
Nuestra Señora de Guanajuato

TOP 10 CITIES

GUANAJUATO, MEXICO

From silver mining to the silver screen, the small city of Guanajuato in the central highlands of Mexico punches above its weight when it comes to topical appeal. The wealth produced by the local seams of silver created a visually stunning cityscape of ornate churches, pretty squares and colourful houses, spread out over the verdant valley in which Guanajuato sits. This natural and man-made beauty caught the eye of Pixar producers who used the city as the real-life basis for their animated Land of the Dead in new movie *Coco*.

FERRANTRAITE © GETTY IMAGES

Population: 172,000
Language: Spanish
Unit of currency: Mexican peso
How to get there: Guanajuato International Airport, 30km west of the city, has flights from major Mexican and some US destinations, including Mexico City, Los Angeles and Atlanta.

TELL ME MORE...

Founded in 1548, Guanajuato is one of Mexico's oldest colonial cities and played a prominent role in the country's fight for independence when, in 1810, a battle between rebels and Spanish troops turned a local miner into a national hero. Nicknamed El Pípila, he singlehandedly stormed the granary in which

'For me, Guanajuato is about rediscovering ancient paths travelled by the silver miners, encountering history, and exploring the hills and mountains that surround us by bicycle, horse, or even better, walking.'
Susana Ojeda Orranti, tourism director, Cacomixtle Tour Company

soldiers had barricaded themselves and gave the rebels a victory. In return, Guanajuato gave him a hilltop statue, which today offers the best view of this Unesco World Heritage city. Other highlights, or lowlights, are the creepy-cool tunnels dug to allow drivers and pedestrians to get around town without navigating the many torturous hills. Back above ground, the city is brimming with architectural wonders such as the lavish 19th-century Teatro Juárez and

ITINERARY
A long weekend in Guanajuato

• Start your visit at **Monumento al Pípila**, a statue of the Mexican hero, with photogenic city views.

• Descend in the funicular and visit the **Museo Iconográfico del Quijote**, a museum dedicated to the best-known creation of Spain's greatest writer, Cervantes. Every October, Guanajuato celebrates the playwright with one of Latin America's biggest arts festivals.

• Wander westwards, past the impressive Teatro Juarez, to see where the artist and political activist was born at the **Museo y Casa de Diego Rivera.**

• Explore **Alhóndiga de Granaditas**, a granary turned War of Independence battleground turned history museum.

• Grab souvenirs and snacks in **Mercado Hidalgo**, the city's largest market.

dozens of museums, including one celebrating another famous local, artist Diego Rivera. The streets fill every evening with locals whose friendliness and enthusiasm stand out even in a country renowned for those attributes.

UNMISSABLE EXPERIENCES

• Take some wine, musicians dressed in 17th-century outfits and Guanajuato's historic alleyways, and you have an *estudiantina*, a mobile street party that takes place every weekend. Practise your Spanish listening to tales of Guanajuato's past and sing along to the popular tunes (everybody knows the 'ay, ay, ay, ay' song, officially entitled *Cielito Lindo*) as

you take an evening stroll through the city's scenic passageways. Fun knows no language barriers. Sign up for one in Jardín de la Unión in the city centre – look for the costumed ticket sellers on weekend afternoons.

TIME YOUR VISIT

A visit to Guanajuato can be enjoyed year-round. Clear, sunny days and warm but never oppressively hot temperatures are the norm. Chilly winter evenings (the city is 2000m up in the mountains, after all) and summer rains make a waterproof jacket a good idea.

• By Clifton Wilkinson

Nineteenth-century Teatro Juarez is a focus of Guanajuato's rich cultural life

Founded as a silver-mining town by the Spanish in the 1500s, Guanajuato's colourful mountain sprawl is now a Unesco World Heritage site

OSLO, NORWAY

Norway's capital has long had to compete with its stylish Nordic neighbours. But Oslo, along with the rest of the nation, is set to toast a landmark event: in 2018, Norway's beloved king and queen celebrate the 50th year of their marriage. Expect fanfare and pageantry aplenty, along with a packed calendar of events – civic, culinary and cultural. As a bonus, Oslo's landmark Opera House is marking its 10th birthday in 2018 with a celebratory season of concerts and performances, so you really couldn't pick a better year to visit.

10

Population: 658,000
Language: Norwegian
Unit of currency: Norwegian krone
How to get there: Oslo's Gardermoen Airport has frequent flights to most European cities, with carriers including Norwegian, SAS and British Airways.

TELL ME MORE...

Oslo's charms have sailed under the Scandinavian radar for far too long, but this compact capital is rising fast. Take the waterfront area of Tjuvholmen: a decade ago this former dockyard felt deeply unloved and industrial, but it's since been reinvented by the city's biggest ever urban renewal project.

It's now home to a host of bars, bistros and ubercool apartment blocks, not to mention the fantastic Astrup Fearnley Museum of Modern Art (designed by Renzo Piano). It's one of several architectural experiments that are gradually reinventing Oslo's skyline: there's a new high-rise district known as the Barcode, plus a striking extension planned for the Vikingskipshuset (Viking Ship Museum). But showing off doesn't really come naturally to Oslo: first and foremost, this is a city to live in, with parks to get lost in, waterways to wander and fjords to kayak – not to mention a coffee culture the equal of Stockholm or Copenhagen.

The clean diagonals of Oslo Opera House have been a fixture since 2007 and are indicative of the city's taste for innovative architecture

ARCHITECT: TARALD LUDEVALL, MATS ANDA © GETTY IMAGES

ITINERARY
A weekend in Oslo

• Begin at the striking concrete-and-glass **Oslo Opera House**, from where it's a short walk to the high-rises of the Barcode.

• Delve into the city to explore the **Nasjonalgalleriet**, brimming with treasures from Monet to Munch to Matisse.

• Head through the tree-lined **Slottsparken** and take a tour of the Royal Palace, followed by the medieval Akershus Festning.

• Walk along the waterfront to the **Astrup Fearnley Museum of Modern Art**, followed by a fjord tour for a different perspective on Oslo's skyline.

• Finish with a night at **The Thief**, Oslo's most architecturally adventurous hotel.

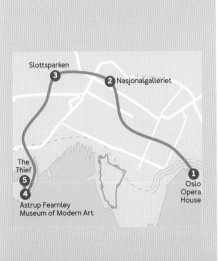

'There's one man in town I go to for my coffee – Tim Wendelboe. He roasts his beans by hand, runs workshops and does superb latte art. He's even won the World Barista Championship!'
Julius Eriksen, bartender

UNMISSABLE EXPERIENCES

• Admire some art at the Munchmuseet, which holds the world's largest collection of Edvard Munch's works – approximately 1100 paintings, 4500 drawings and 18,000 prints, although the artist's showpiece, *The Scream*, is displayed at the Nasjonalgalleriet (National Gallery) downtown.

• Go shopping in Grünerløkka, a favourite hangout for Oslo's hipsters, who come here to sip small-batch beer, buy vintage togs and browse for classic vinyl.

• Step back in time at the Vikingskipshuset, home to two beautifully preserved Viking longships, the *Oseberg* and *Gokstad*, dug up from Oslofjord 1100 years after they were buried during a chieftain's funeral ceremony. Fragments of a third ship, the *Tune*, are also on show.

TIME YOUR VISIT

In Oslo, every season has its charm. Summertime is best for outdoor adventures such as bike-riding and kayaking, while spring and autumn are ideal for city wandering. Winter brings frequent snow and festive markets – it's an atmospheric time of year, but you'll need to wrap up warm.

• By Oliver Berry

THE
TRAVEL
EDIT

Best value destinations / Best culture trips for families
Best new openings / Best new places to stay

BEST VALUE DESTINATIONS

If you're looking to wander frugally or save on a visit to pricier big-hitters, then our list of good-value getaways is the place to start.

↘ 1 TALLINN, ESTONIA

Estonia's capital is compact, fashionable and terrific value. Explore one of Eastern Europe's loveliest old towns on foot for free, stay in good-value dorms, guesthouses or private homes, and take in Baltic Sea views and a superb panorama of the city from the flat roof of the vast Linnahall (one of Tallinn's best free things to do). Connected by budget flights from around Europe, the city isn't a secret – but if you want a taste of Tallinn to yourself then head to Kalamaja, a fast-changing neighbourhood home to Telliskivi Creative City. The food trucks here offer Instagrammable fill-ups that won't tax your wallet.

As well as European flight routes, Tallinn is connected by ferry to Helsinki, Stockholm and St Petersburg; see timetables on www. portoftallinn.com/passenger-ship-schedules.

2 LANZAROTE, CANARY ISLANDS

Over the past decade, in-the-know independent travellers are increasingly heading to Lanzarote. Awaiting them is a well-developed infrastructure that makes it a doddle to find affordable lodgings, food and car rental. There's plenty of no-nonsense holiday fun, but Lanzarote also revels in its uniqueness. The moon-like scenery of Parque Nacional de Timanfaya, unspoilt beaches of Órzola and black-sand wineries of La Geria reward those who come here for more than a traditional seaside break. In one small package you can explore César Manrique's artistic and architectural footprint, follow stunning hiking trails, and enjoy unexpected and jaw-dropping views along many drives around Lanzarote.

César Manrique's buildings and artworks are big-ticket items, so aim to see them early or late in the day to avoid crowds.

↘ 3 ARIZONA, USA

For affordable and accessible adventures in Arizona, aim for simple roadside motels, then camp and hike. Visit Saguaro National Park on a day or overnight trip from Tucson. Over in Organ Pipe Cactus National Monument you'll find fewer fellow visitors to compete with for views. Shoulder season unlocks great value: visit the South Rim of the Grand Canyon from March to May and September to October for cooler temperatures and lighter crowds. For the less crowded North Rim, go in May or October. Aim for Scottsdale's spas and golf courses between June and August. Sure, it's hot by day – but there's always the poolside for those sizzling hours. *The desert climate and high altitude of many Arizona attractions make for chilly nights: pack accordingly, especially if camping.*

THE TRAVEL EDIT
BEST IN TRAVEL 2018

↘ 4 LA PAZ, BOLIVIA

FILIPPO BACCI © GETTY IMAGES

Spectacularly situated at 3660m, La Paz is one of South America's best value places to linger, whether you're keen on acclimatising, learning Spanish or simply enjoying the colourful street life and Andean setting. Budget-conscious travellers can get by on less than US$30 a day, eating at unforgettable markets and taking hiking and biking trips. La Paz also has a fast-emerging yet affordable upscale scene, epitomised by superb dining at places such as Gustu, founded by Noma's Claus Meyer. Boutique hotels and hip coffee joints are popping up too, all at lower prices than their equivalents elsewhere. Move fast: La Paz is on the rise.
Reach La Paz's El Alto International Airport – the world's highest, at 4061m – by indirect flights from Miami and Washington DC.

GARY LATHAM © GETTY IMAGES/CULTURA EXCLUSIVE

↘ 5 POLAND

Poland somehow manages to remain affordable and relatively under-visited. Sure, Kraków grabs the crowds, but you can explore here for less than in Prague or Berlin. Beyond Kraków is a roll-call of Europe's least-appreciated highlights. In the north, explore Gdańsk's rebuilt old town and haunting coastal scenery. Elsewhere, Lublin, Toruń and Tarnów's historical beauty (free from large numbers of visitors) can form the basis of a wonderful week. If you have more time, consider exploring the mountain playground around budget-friendly Zakopane or bison-spotting in Białowieża National Park. Inexpensive train and bus connections, keenly priced food and beer, plus budget places to stay complete the picture.

Point-to-point rail travel in Poland is good value, meaning a rail pass isn't generally needed. Book in advance for the best fares. www.polrail.com

BEST VALUE DESTINATIONS

THE
TRAVEL
EDIT

BEST IN
TRAVEL
2o18

↗ 6 ESSAOUIRA, MOROCCO

Love Morocco? Been to Marrakesh? Us too. If you're seeking another, still affordable side of this safe slice of north Africa then Essaouira might just be the place for you. A popular day trip from Marrakesh itself, Essaouira can now be reached direct by low-cost flights from the UK and France. The walled city's narrow alleyways, traditional hammams and medina pile on the sensory delight. The breeze allows for superb wind and kitesurfing, as well as bracing beach strolls. Characterful riads are affordable, especially if you're travelling with family or a group. Best of all, the food is sensational even on a low budget, in particular the just-landed seafood.

Overland, Essaouira is around a three-hour bus ride from Marrakesh and about four hours more from Casablanca.

↘ 7 UNITED KINGDOM

While the UK government busies itself with Brexit, travellers can reap the rewards. The immediate result of 2016's referendum on EU membership was the pound weakening against pretty much all currencies: good news for those of us planning a trip to London, not traditionally a paradise for frugal adventurers. Make the exchange rate work even harder by aiming for Devon, Cornwall and big-ticket cities such as Bath, York and Edinburgh (they're cheaper outside school holidays like Easter, July and August).

Keep an eye on currency fluctuations, but the most likely scenario is that the UK stays affordable to international visitors – at least until a true picture of the post-Brexit landscape emerges. *Check exchange rates at www.oanda.com/ currency, where you can also find useful tools including pocket-sized conversion tables.*

ANDREW PICKETT © GETTY IMAGES/VISITBRITAIN

↘ 8 BAJA CALIFORNIA, MEXICO

It's the world's second-longest peninsula; but for many, visiting Baja California still means a quick hop over the border into Tijuana or Tecate – meaning there's 1200km of less-explored territory. True, prices can be higher here than in other parts of Mexico due to the relative remoteness of Baja. But if you're coming from the US, you'll be saving money by travelling here. In the north, the wine route through the Valle de Guadalupe is like Napa but a lot cheaper. Meanwhile, towns such as Todos Santos, Loreto, San Ignacio, Mulegé and La Paz are authentically Mexican and feature great-value accommodation.

To beat the queues at the Tijuana border crossing, try entering at Tecate. This route also offers better access to the Ruta del Vino.

↙ 9 JACKSONVILLE, FLORIDA, USA

Jax, as locals call it, hasn't drawn international praise like other destinations in Florida – despite 35km of beaches, surfing, art and live music. There are long stretches of the St Johns River, the Intracoastal Waterway and America's largest urban park system to explore on foot, by bike or, best of all, on a guided kayak tour. Barbecue joints and beachside cafes offer good-value and family-friendly dining, while a pint of craft beer at one of eight local breweries can be priced as low as $3.50. Not only is Jacksonville affordable for sleeping (with the lowest hotel rates in the state), but you can feel as if you're discovering somewhere new.

Jacksonville is the largest city in the continental USA by area, meaning that a car is necessary to get around.

↗ 10 HUNAN, CHINA

Hunan's highlights come thick and fast. At Zhangjiajie, an amazing sandstone canyon with almost 250 bizarrely shaped peaks, the world's longest glass bridge opened in 2016. Another don't-miss is Fenghuang, a stunning historic town that quite literally hangs over the Tuo River. If you're not sold yet, the provincial capital Changsha happened to be Mao Zedong's home town. This being China, costs can be very low indeed: budget meals and accommodation are in the sub-$10 range, and even slap-up servings of fiery Hunan cuisine in the flashiest Changsha digs cost not much more than double that.

Changsha Airport has a maglev link to Changsha South railway station. From here, high-speed rail services connect with major cities.

• By Tom Hall

BEST CULTURE TRIPS FOR FAMILIES

Travel with your kids can broaden their understanding of other people and societies. Expand the whole family's cultural horizons on these inspiring trips.

1 OMAN

Oman is an excellent and gentle introduction to the Middle East. Elegant Muscat (where buildings have to adhere to strict rules of traditional design) can give your kids an insight into a centuries-old way of life: join a dhow cruise or just sit and watch fishermen at work. Beyond the capital, there are mud-brick villages to explore, forts and castles to battle in, and souks where your kids can hone those haggling skills... before rounding off the trip with some relaxing time at the beach. However, the thing your family will most remember is the embracing welcome of the Omanis you meet. *The best time to travel to Oman is between October and April; June to August tend to be scorching hot.*

2 NORWAY

Scandinavian culture has been on trend for travellers for many years, but funky design and cutting-edge gastronomy are not attractions you necessarily associate with children. However, thanks to family-friendly resorts and the fact that kids under eight go free, Norway is increasingly popular for families introducing their children to that popular Scandinavian activity: skiing. Throw in Viking museums,

THE
TRAVEL
EDIT
BEST IN
TRAVEL
2018

theme parks with trolls and fairy palaces, elk safaris and dog-sledding (all delivered with a strong dose of properly child-focused service), and a trip to Norway will convert your kids to all things Scandi.

Don't forget that distances between towns in Norway are huge – plan carefully to avoid too many long travelling days.

↙ 3 NAMIBIA

If you want to introduce your children to life in southern Africa, Namibia is the perfect starting point. There are many interesting and affordable accommodation options for families, roads are well maintained and the healthcare is good. While Namibia makes the tourist headlines for wildlife watching in Etosha National Park, the famous sand dunes at Sossusvlei and adrenaline sports in Swakopmund (all of which can be easily adapted for kids), it's also an excellent place to learn about modern tribal culture – plan ahead to join a thoughtfully organised guided visit to a Himba settlement.

Safari companies generally only take children over eight; it's worth looking at self-drive options if you are travelling with younger children.

4 MEXICO

From exploring Aztec ruins to running around the square of an old colonial town, learning about Frida Kahlo's art to eating corn-on-the-cob from a street vendor, Mexico is an exuberant and friendly assault on all the senses – and it's one your kids will never forget. Take the tempo up in fun-loving Mexico City, relax with locals on the beach in Tulum, or ride a train through the Copper Canyon (which is also home to an adventure park with seven zip-lines!). Families always receive a warm welcome here.

If you can time your visit for the start of November, the Day of the Dead festival gives a unique and fascinating insight into Mexican culture.

5 EMILIA-ROMAGNA, ITALY

Children love Italy. There's pizza, pasta and the world's best ice cream to start with, plus a culture that welcomes kids everywhere. But how do you escape the crowds and really get to know both modern and historic Italy? Step in Emilia-Romagna: there's Parma ham and parmesan for your little foodies, the mosaics of Ravenna for budding artists, and photogenic Bologna, which has a past to fascinate history buffs. And that's not to leave out beach culture in Rimini, more incredible art in Ferrara and the Unesco World Heritage site of Modena's Cathedral. Phew!

With a mock-up of a Roman canal, 3D films and interactive displays, the Museo della Storia di Bologna brings city history to life. www.genusbononiae.it

7 AMSTERDAM, THE NETHERLANDS

Famously laid-back (and possibly better known for more adult pursuits), Amsterdam is a fun place to bring your family. Of course, you can do serious science at the hands-on NEMO Museum, serious art (the Rijksmuseum has excellent family tours) and even more serious history: the Anne Frank House needs no introduction and, at the Verzetsmuseum Junior, you can learn the stories of four Dutch children under occupation. But you can also take a pedalo on the canals, eat stacks of delicious Dutch pancakes, ride a famous Dutch bike and burn off loads of energy in the Vondelpark. *Both the Van Gogh Museum and Rembrandt House Museum have child-friendly activities.*

8 NASHVILLE, TENNESSEE, USA

Could there be a better way to introduce your family to country-music culture than a weekend in Nashville? Sure, alcohol-infused evenings in a honky-tonk might not be the most child-friendly pastime, but there are many other ways to explore the city's rich artistic heritage. The Country Music Hall of Fame has interactive exhibits, listening booths and the chance to make your own song as a family; the Johnny Cash Museum has films to keep little ones engaged; and lastly, kids love seeing the city with the Music City Trolley Hop-On Hop-Off. *Explore another side of Nashville at the Belle Meade Plantation, a mansion with a fascinating history and grounds geared for rambling in.* bellemeadeplantation.com

↗ 6 ORKNEY, SCOTLAND

The adventurous journey required to reach Orkney will kick-start your family's immersion into the islands' fascinating cultural heritage. Once off the ferry you have 5000 years of history to explore, from the ruins of a Neolithic village at Skara Brae and the Viking legacy at Kirkwall, to the role played by Orkney in World War II, which is well documented at the Scapa Flow Visitor Centre. When everyone's had enough of the history lessons there are beaches to tear around, super-sweet Scottish tablet to be devoured and even a good chance of a dance to some traditional folk music. *Want to keep the kids busy on the beach? Get them to find cowrie shells or 'groatie buckies'.*

9 BRISBANE, AUSTRALIA

For a taste of the uber-relaxed, outdoorsy, barbecue-loving culture that is quintessentially Australian, a trip to Brisbane hits the right notes for those with kids. Splash around on man-made Streets Beach (perfect for small swimmers) or let off steam in the tree-house playground at New Farm Park. Relax with a BBQ in the riverside South Bank Parklands before checking out koalas at nearby Lone Pine Sanctuary. For a taste of ancient Australian culture, there's Aboriginal art in the Queensland Art Gallery and Gallery of Modern Art (QAGOMA), which runs sessions for children.

Get your kids ready for their artistic adventure in Brisbane on QAGOMA's kids website. www.qagoma.qld.gov.au/learn/kids

↘ 10 KYOTO, JAPAN

A visit to Kyoto is a great first step for Western kids to understand Japanese culture, as there are plenty of distractions if the cultural overload is too much. Take Fushimi Inari-Taisha with its famous *torii* gates: it's a fascinating example of a traditional shrine but there's space to burn off energy. Or the Shōren-in temple, which has carp to count and a bamboo forest to explore in its landscaped gardens. And hit the 400-year-old Nishiki Market: you can buy all sorts of Japanese delicacies before tipping out into a shopping mall for a plate of something more familiar.

Picnic in the Kyoto Botanical Garden. In March or April, the cherry blossom can last longer here.

• By Imogen Hall

BEST NEW OPENINGS

Think you've seen it all? Refresh your bucket list with these incredible new openings and experiences coming in 2018.

↗ 1 NINJA TOURISM, JAPAN

Japan will continue to revive the ancient art of ninja with a wealth of activities high-kicking off in 2018. Visitors can choose from two specialised ninja tours with stays in famous sites such as the province of Iga, the location of two major sacred grounds for the discipline and some of its most famous schools. Tokyo will soon be home to a new Ninja Museum, as well as a Ninja Academy where visitors can train under the supervision of the 'last ninja', Jinichi Kawakami. If you're good enough to pass all the classes, you'll go on to become a certified ninja. *The Japan Ninja Council is leading the way on this ancient discipline's revitalisation, and will publish all updates on ninja-official.com.*

2 OCEAN CAY MARINE RESERVE, THE BAHAMAS

Work is underway to transform an old industrial site into a thriving new marine reserve and private island. Guests of MSC Cruises will soon be able to explore the Ocean Cay Marine Reserve's sandy beaches and calm lagoons, or relax at tiki bars and dedicated family areas. Tourists aren't the only ones to benefit: the reserve is being designed to promote the growth of coral and marine life, and more than 80 indigenous plants will be grown on the rejuvenated and pristine island. *The island is set to welcome cruise guests from November 2018; browse voyages to Ocean Cay Marine Reserve on www.msccruises.com.*

3 DIVING THE *TITANIC*, NEWFOUNDLAND, CANADA

Adventurers can now take the plunge to the world's most famous shipwreck on an unforgettable eight-day expedition from Newfoundland. Travelling with Blue Marble Private and a crew of experts, you'll explore the wreck of the RMS *Titanic* in a submersible craft at depths of almost 4000m, and get a glimpse of the ship's most iconic sights, including the famous staircase. This subterranean odyssey is one of the rarest travel experiences in the world and places are limited.

Blue Marble's Titanic dives commence in 2018 and run until 2019; book the dive of a lifetime through www.bluemarbleprivate.com.

4 FLIGHTS FROM ARGENTINA TO ANTARCTICA

From January 2018 there'll be a whole new way to discover one of the most untouched regions in the world: Argentina's state-owned airline LADE will begin the first ever regular commercial flights to the frozen continent. Instead of taking a cruise (and battling seasickness), intrepid visitors can hop aboard weekly flights from Ushuaia in Argentina to Antarctica's Marambio Base, taking just 90 minutes. The base is principally used for science and research, but will be developed and expanded to include accommodation for tourists along with improvements geared towards commercial flights.

Weekly flights are set to commence in January 2018. Keep an eye on LADE's website (www.lade.com.ar) for more details.

↘ 5 VESSEL GALLERY, NEW YORK CITY, USA

New York City is about to get a new icon. Vessel will be a spectacular climbable installation in the middle of the new Hudson Yards development, which is set to regenerate the city's Far West Side (previously an industrial zone). The glinting copper structure will be the centrepiece of the Public Square and Gardens and will comprise 154 interconnecting flights of stairs in a geometric pattern. Visitors can ascend the 45m-high structure via the mile-long network of pathways, with each staircase providing a slightly different perspective on the brand new neighbourhood below.

Vessel (www.hudsonyardsnewyork.com) will open to the public in autumn 2018.

© FORBES MASSIE-HEATHERWICK STUDIO

↘ 6 L'ATELIER DES LUMIÈRES, PARIS, FRANCE

Paris' historic art scene will get a breath of fresh air when l'Atelier des Lumières opens to the public. Devoted to immersive art experiences, each year the Atelier will showcase a major exhibition offering a digital perspective on one of art's biggest names, allowing you to step inside the world's most famous artworks. Meanwhile, a smaller exhibit will probe a more contemporary theme. Covering a whopping 2000 sq m, l'Atelier des Lumières is set to utterly transform a 19th-century factory, with innovative, 8m-high projections cloaking its walls.

The grand unveiling is at 38/40 rue Saint-Maur in April 2018; keep an eye on its progress at www.atelier-lumieres.com.

7 SCIENCE GALLERY, LONDON, UK; DETROIT, USA

The Science Gallery has been delighting and enthralling visitors in Dublin since 2008. In 2018, it will open a new, permanent base in London and start a three-year project in Detroit. The UK instalment will be next to London Bridge and house rotating thematic exhibitions exploring life's big questions. All displays will be participatory in nature, and your responses could even feed into the gallery's academic research. Across the pond, Detroit's temporary offering in Michigan State University is geared towards pioneering new research methods to students and academics.

London Science Gallery will open in 2018 and will be free to visit. For more on its opening date visit london.sciencegallery.com.

ARTWORK © GUSTAV KLIMT. © CULTURESPACES, DR

9 ULYSSES CENTRE, DUBLIN, IRELAND

Ireland's formidable literary history will be the focal point of a new tourist centre in historic Newman House, right in the heart of Georgian Dublin. James Joyce attended lectures in the building and the centre's immersive and interactive exhibition will have a special focus on his work, as well as celebrating the other members of Ireland's impressive literary hall of fame. There will also be rotating exhibitions on more contemporary figures, plus the centre will be open for lectures and performances.

The Ulysses Centre (www.ucdfoundation.ie/ ulysses_centre) is set to open in Dublin in autumn 2018.

10 AUGUST MOON DRIVE-IN, NASHVILLE, USA

Drive all the way back to the 1960s with this new 4180 sq m entertainment space in Music City. Inside the mini indoor theme park, you'll be transported to a perfect summer night, complete with starry sky and chirping crickets. Take a seat in your choice of classic cars and watch the latest blockbusters or rare classics on North America's largest non-IMAX cinema screen. It's not pure nostalgia: the owners promise ground-breaking technology and even live actors to add personalisation and interaction with the audience.

This movie-lover's marvel is due to open in spring 2018 in East Nashville; get the latest on www.augustmoondrivein.com.

• By AnneMarie McCarthy

↗ 8 DIRECT FLIGHTS FROM AUSTRALIA TO EUROPE

Say goodbye to layovers with the first direct flight linking Australia to Europe. The new Qantas flight will link Perth to London in 17 hours, making it one of the longest passenger flights in the world. The airline is aiming to make the flight as comfortable as possible for its economy passengers, including using the Dreamliner 787 for the route, an aircraft designed to decrease turbulence and improve air quality. It's also a great excuse for Europeans to explore Australia's most remote city.

The first service will run in March 2018 and tickets are available to book through www.qantas.com.

BEST NEW PLACES TO STAY

Whether you're looking to splash cash or save on your stay, there are some extraordinary new places to lay your head in 2018. The only issue? The excitement may keep you awake.

↘ 1 SILO HOTEL, SOUTH AFRICA

Built within the lift tower of an old grain silo in Cape Town's V&A Waterfront, this incredible boutique hotel is as stunning as the views it offers of Table Mountain. The Silo juxtaposes modernity with history, featuring geodesic windows bulging out of the 1920s industrial concrete exterior. And as the much-hyped Zeitz Museum of Contemporary Art Africa (MOCAA) has opened downstairs, it just gets better. *MOCAA's sculpture garden will be accessible from a weighbridge on the Silo's sixth floor.* www.theroyalportfolio.com/the-silo

2 FLOATING CAPSULE HOTEL, JAPAN

In 2015, Huis Ten Bosch created the world's first hotel staffed by robots, and in late 2017 it is scheduled to complete its new floating capsule hotel. The two-storey spheres, complete with beds under a glass dome, will travel slowly across a 6km stretch of water during the night, bringing guests to a new island adventure resort.

Huis Ten Bosch is located in the city of Sasebo, Nagasaki Prefecture. english.huistenbosch.co.jp

↗ 3 THOUSAND LAKES LODGE, AUSTRALIA

The chance to explore the rugged and isolated beauty of the Unesco-listed Tasmanian Wilderness World Heritage Area is now a step closer, thanks to this freshly opened lodge. Transformed from a former training facility for Antarctic expeditions, the nine-room Thousand Lakes Lodge is an incredibly welcoming (and warming) place to base yourself for hiking, fishing, mountain biking and wildlife watching on the beautiful highland plains.

The low-impact eco-lodge is a 90-minute drive from Launceston in northern Tasmania. www.thousandlakeslodge.com.au

↗ 4 JAM HOTEL, BELGIUM

When Jean-Michel André, the brains behind Château de la Poste, Chelton and Le Berger hotels, combined forces with architect Olivia Gustot to transform the former St Luke School of Architecture in Brussels, the result was

ALICE HANSEN © THOUSAND LAKES LODGE

DAN GRAINIC | JAM HOTEL

bound to be exceptional. Urban tones abound, with exposed brick, concrete and plywood throughout. The 78 rooms are topped out with an attractive bar and lengthy rooftop pool and terrace.

There's the 18-bed Giga dorm (€18), Super singles (€49) and other private rooms for groups ranging from two to six people. www.jamhotel.be

© ASILIA

5 MOSS HOTEL, ICELAND

The steaming Blue Lagoon is Iceland's most famed sight, and this year it will be possible to wake up with a spectacular view over it. Powered by sustainable energy from geothermal activity, this modern and minimalist luxury hotel sits atop moss-covered lava flows that date back to 1226. And, of course, a Blue Lagoon hotel wouldn't be complete without a subterranean spa – the Lava Cove.

The Lagoon Suite features access to a private portion of the lagoon. hotel.bluelagoon.com

6 THE SILL, UK

Youth hostels are rarely gleaming, stylish sculptures of glass and steel. And it's not often one forms part of a unique 'discovery centre'. But at historic Hadrian's Wall in Northumberland, The Sill is replete with space

for exhibitions, plays and music events. Rooms sleep two, three or four people, and have access to a kitchen, chill zones, wi-fi and some of the starriest skies around.

The whole complex is powered by renewable energy. Beds (with breakfast) start from £21. www.yha.org.uk

7 AWASI IGUAZÚ, ARGENTINA

Building on its pioneering properties in the Atacama and Patagonia, Awasi has created a wonderful 12-villa lodge just 15 minutes from the legendary Iguazú Falls. Perched on stilts to reduce environmental impact, and well spaced in dense jungle along the banks of the Iguazú River, villas feature private plunge pools, outdoor showers and large living areas.

Each villa has a 4WD and private guide to explore the area. www.awasiguazu.com

8 THE ROBEY, USA

Like a thick slice of Art Deco pie, this wedge-shaped hotel towers over an area of Chicago that eats, drinks and breathes art and culture – namely the neighbourhoods of Wicker Park and Bucktown. The eclectic energy on the streets carries right up to The Robey's 13th-floor lounge, which offers uninterrupted 180-degree views of the city's skyline. *Late check-outs, transport links aplenty and rooms from US$175... happy days (and nights). www.therobey.com*

↖ 9 THE HIGHLANDS CAMP, TANZANIA

While other travellers queue to enter the wildlife haven of Ngorongoro, Africa's most famous crater, guests at Asila's Highlands Camp will awake inside a remote part of the conservation area. Taking glamping to a new level, this eco-conscious camp's eight large rooms are quilted, cocoon-like domes with unforgettable views over the African wilderness. And Asila's long-term relationship with local Maasai carries

over to rich and meaningful cultural experiences for guests, too. *Wildlife drives, hikes and meals are all included. www.asiliaafrica.com*

↘ 10 NULL STERN, SWITZERLAND

Five stars? Try no stars (well, except those above your head), and no walls for that matter. The brainchild of twin concept artists Patrik and Frank Riklin, the Null Stern is nothing but a beautiful bed in the middle of the Swiss wilderness. The original 'Alpine Room' sold out quickly in 2017, but 25 more beds in secret Swiss locations will crop up in 2018. *Add your name to the waiting list before it's too late. www.nullsternhotel.ch*
• By Matt Phillips

TOP
TRENDS

Destination races / Vegetarian & vegan travel / Exploratory cruises

Cross-generational travel / Private islands for all!

DESTINATION RACES

Forget Boston, London and New York marathons, these races will take you (and your legs) further than you've ever dreamed! Walk, run, cycle, swim or crawl, it's all about crossing the finish line.

1 SAFARICOM MARATHON, KENYA

With nothing physically separating you from 26 lions, 137 rhinos, 182 giraffes and 1160 zebras, this marathon is a run on the wild side. Curious giraffes may occasionally keep stride with you; 140 armed rangers and three spotter helicopters work to ensure your path is clear of Africa's apex predators. Heat, hills and an average elevation of 1700m add to the challenge.

Lewa Wildlife Conservancy is a four-hour drive or 45-minute flight from Nairobi. The race takes place in late June. www.safaricommarathon.com

↗ 2 NORTH POLE MARATHON

There are cool marathons, and then there are cool marathons. Pack *very* warmly, journey to Svalbard in Norway and board a jet to the polar ice cap for a run like no other. You may want to hit this floating 42.2km ice course hard, but the elements (and snow suits and boots) will require a slower approach than usual.

The hefty €16,000 entry fee includes return flights from Svalbard to the North Pole camp and helicopter tours. www.npmarathon.com

3 MARATHON DU MÉDOC, FRANCE

Reaching any marathon finish line is a challenge, but with numerous wine stops at Bordeaux's heralded vineyards, the Marathon du Médoc provides a unique physical test. We say 'numerous' as most competitors can't recall how many pit stops they made! Cheese, pâté and other local treats line the route.

This early-September race starts and finishes in Pauillac, accessible from Bordeaux by train, bus and shuttles. www.marathondumedoc.com

4 MARATHON DES SABLES, MOROCCO

Fancy running the equivalent of almost six marathons in a week, including 80km in one go? OK. Now try it in the soft sands of the Sahara. Oh, and turn up the thermostat past 50°C and carry your week's worth of food (minimum 2000 calories per day) and supplies with you. This multi-stage event will push you to your limit and beyond, guaranteed.

Covering around 250km in southern Morocco, the Marathon des Sables takes place in early to mid-April. www.marathondessables.com

↗ 5 GRAND TO GRAND ULTRA, USA

The first self-supported multi-stage race in the US, this 273km ultra marathon takes competitors from the north rim of the iconic Grand Canyon to the top of the Grand Staircase, one of the planet's most celebrated geological formations. In between, the high-desert route crosses red sand dunes, runs through slot canyons and skirts towering buttes, delicate hoodoos and vast mesas.

It's 320km from Las Vegas international airport to the race base in Kanab, Utah. www.g2gultra.com

6 INCA TRAIL MARATHON, PERU

In ancient times, highly skilled and physically fit messengers (*chasquis*) used to relay-run encrypted posts (*quipus*) between settlements of the Inca empire. Attempt one of the most famous routes yourself by taking on this marathon. The finish line? Machu Picchu! With 3000m of elevation gain, 3300m of descent and a high point of 4215m, this is a challenge for the ages.

In 2018, Andes Adventures (www. andesadventures.com) run the event in June and August, and Erik's Adventures (www.eriksadventures.com) in July.

↗ 7 ESCAPE FROM ALCATRAZ TRIATHLON, USA

They say no one ever escaped from Alcatraz. Want to give it a go? Dive off the prison island into San Francisco Bay's chilly (and some say shark-filled) waters for a 2.4km swim to shore, before a warm-up run to your bicycle at Marina Green. Pedal 29km through the hills of the city and Golden Gate Park, then run 13km for home at Baker Beach Battery.

The mid-June race is capped at 2000 entrants so age-group amateurs will need to rely on the draw for entry. www.escapealcatraztri.com

→ 8 GREAT WALL MARATHON, CHINA

They don't call it great for nothing. This fantastic structure is impressive on all fronts, and the Great Wall Marathon certainly does it justice. The route, which includes 5164 stone steps, is certainly no walk in the park – but the views of surrounding hills, villages and the wall itself may just take away some of the pain.

Held on 19 May this year, the race starts from the Huangyaguan fortress, some 120km east of Běijīng. www.great-wall-marathon.com

9 WHOLE EARTH MAN V HORSE MARATHON, WALES

Which is faster over a long distance, human or horse? It was this question in a Welsh pub that spawned this race in 1980. Since then the two have been doing battle over challenging terrain, though it took 25 races before a man on foot finally outpaced his counterpart on horseback. The race distance has varied, but should be around 35km in 2018.

Start and end point Llanwrtyd Wells is a three-hour train journey north of Cardiff. The race takes place in mid-June. www.green-events.co.uk/?mvh_main

→ 10 OUTBACK MARATHON, AUSTRALIA

Go 'walkabout' in the Australian outback at this marathon in the shadow of legendary Uluru. The relatively flat course is along the area's red dirt fire access trails, though the occasional sand dune will put a dent in your stride (as will views of Kata Tjuta and Uluru).

The organisers offer various race/ accommodation packages, ranging from three to six days (entry-only participation is not possible). Ayers Rock Airport is nearby. www.australianoutbackmarathon.com

• By Matt Phillips

TOP
TRENDS

BEST IN
TRAVEL
2018

VEGETARIAN & VEGAN TRAVEL

More and more people are developing a taste for vegan and vegetarian dining with benefits to their health, the planet and, of course, the animals. Travel the less traditional culinary road at these veg-friendly eateries across the globe, from newcomers to old classics.

1 BOULDIN CREEK CAFÉ, AUSTIN, TEXAS, USA

Think Texas is all about boots and barbecue? It's time to take a second look. In the boho-loving city of Austin, Bouldin Creek Café has a neighbourhood vibe, friendly staff and a menu of Tex-Mex hits such as vegan enchiladas, fajitas with portobellos and a much-lauded veggie burger. This mostly vegan spot also has great outdoor dining and people-watching. *Breakfast is served all day, perfect for late-start mornings after taking in Austin's live music scene. bouldincreekcafe.com*

2 DATE & THYME, KEY WEST, FLORIDA, USA

Until recently, it was easier to stumble across a drag show cabaret than a vegetarian restaurant in free-spirited Key West. All that's changed due to arrivals such as Date & Thyme, a laid-back vegan cafe and market set in a converted petrol station. You can eat al fresco on the front terrace among wandering chickens – they rule the streets of the island! *www.helpyourselffoods.com. Across the street is Salt Island Provisions, a crafty little shop and gallery that sells one-of-a-kind gourmet salts.*

→ 3 THE SOUL KITCHEN, PARIS, FRANCE

A short stroll from the hilltop basilica of Sacré-Cœur, the Soul Kitchen is a standout among Montmartre's charming cafes. It's run by three women whose love of food infuses the market-driven dishes (half the menu is vegetarian). If you can't stay for a meal, stop by for strong coffee and vegan cookies, with a side of daydreaming beside the bay window. *There's a cupboard full of board games tucked away in the corner for those drizzly afternoons. www.facebook.com/soulkitchenparis*

4 VEGETARIANO SOCIAL CLUBE, RIO DE JANEIRO, BRAZIL

In Rio's restaurant-lined Leblon district, you can feast on a vegan version of *feijoada*, one of Brazil's signature dishes – and it's just as decadent as the traditional recipe. Chefs cook up the popular stew with black beans and smoked tempeh (rather than pork). It's served on Wednesdays and Sundays, and goes down nicely with a passionfruit caipirinha or three.

Take a stroll along Leblon's beachside boulevard, closed to traffic on Sundays all the way to Leme. vegetarianosocialclube.com.br

5 CAT BAR, BARCELONA, SPAIN

Burgers and craft beer are a winning combo, all the more so when they're made with Earth-friendly ingredients. At this atmospheric little haunt in Barcelona's El Born district, the vegan burgers are large, creatively topped and sinfully good. The beers, made in Catalonia (the 'Cat' part of the equation), showcase the burgeoning microbrew scene of this distinctive region.

A few blocks away is the 14th-century Santa Maria del Mar, one of Barcelona's most impressive churches. www.catbarcat.com

VALERIA BISMAR © LA PANTHÈRE VERTE

6 BE KIND TO ANIMALS THE MOON, BAGAN, MYANMAR

Never mind the heart-warming (but baffling) name of this vegetarian restaurant near the ancient temples of Bagan. What matters is the delicious cooking, made with the freshest ingredients and served in a peaceful open-air setting. Come for pumpkin curry with ginger, chapati wraps and creamy banana lassi. Leave room for homemade ice cream for dessert.

Find it about 300m north of Ananda Temple, and 300m east of the Tharabar Gate.

⬐ 7 LA PANTHÈRE VERTE, MONTRÉAL, CANADA

Now found in a growing number of locations, the 'Green Panther' makes it easier than ever to eat sustainably in Montréal. One bite of the famed falafel sandwich, and you'll realise why this vegan chain has become so popular. It is also one of the greenest restaurants in town, with locally sourced organic ingredients and environmentally responsible practices.

The Latin Quarter branch also serves beers on tap from Beau's, a small Canadian brewer that uses only organic ingredients. thegreenpanther.com

8 SALSA VERDE, ÉVORA, PORTUGAL

Pedro, the owner of Salsa Verde, lays out the welcome mat for out-of-towners who stumble upon his cheerfully decorated restaurant. He happily guides diners through his ever-changing menu of Alentejan delicacies prepared with vegetarian ingredients. Here, the garlic and olive oil-soaked bread dish *migas* is made with mushrooms (not meat), and casseroles are baked with spinach or tofu (rather than cod).

After a filling meal, walk it off amid flowerbeds and birdsong in the nearby Jardim Público (Public Gardens). www.salsa-verde.org

9 HILTL, ZÜRICH, SWITZERLAND

Eating mindfully is all the rage these days, but meat-free dining isn't a new idea. Take Hiltl, the world's oldest vegetarian restaurant, which opened its doors in 1898. Run by the same family for four generations, its extensive menu offers more than 100 vegetarian and vegan dishes, from cuisines spanning the globe.

During the summer, Hiltl operates two restaurants on lovely Lake Zürich at the resorts of Mythenquai and Kilchberg. www.hiltl.ch

10 OKUTAN KIYOMIZU, KYOTO, JAPAN

It's not easy to be vegan in Japan. But Kyoto, with age-old reverence for traditionally made tofu, has some mouthwatering options. Okutan Kiyomizu has been preparing tofu for temple monks since 1635. It's a hushed place where you sit at low tables, lingering over *yudofu* (tofu in a clay pot with vegetables). Ask for vegan or vegetarian; each mouthful is a delight.

The restaurant sits within the garden of Chōshō-in outside Nanzen-ji, one of Japan's most important Zen temples.

• By Regis St Louis

EXPLORATORY CRUISES

An all-you-can-eat buffet dinner aboard a tricked-out ocean liner isn't the only way to get your sea legs. Small-ship expedition cruises are on the rise as adventurous travellers search for immersive ways to discover far-flung destinations.

Cruises have been bucket list fodder since *The Love Boat* first sailed from television screens into living rooms during the 1970s. These days, the mere word 'cruise' conjures visions of mainstream mega ships that are as much resorts as they are modes of transportation. But exploratory cruises are bucking the trend.

From alluring Polar voyages to deep jungle journeys, these cruises are 'explorations' in the literal sense, as they chart courses to rarely visited lands. But there's also an element of inner exploration, elicited by thoughtfully crafted itineraries: activities on- and off-board can enable deeper personal reflection and more intentional engagement with nature and local culture. The result is a truly transformative travel experience.

Thanks to a flotilla of ships navigating the world's waters, travellers are able to explore lands seen by few others with the ease, convenience and security that a cruise – both as a means of movement and an experiential staging ground – can provide.

Some exploratory cruises show popular destinations in a new light, but most specialise in reaching remote places: often, small-ship cruising is the only way to access precious and protected lands. But gone are the days when 'adventure' was synonymous with 'roughing it'. Most conveniences come as standard with on-board accommodation, and amenities range from humble and comfy to superbly sybarite.

But don't count on lazing the days away by a pool, or sipping cocktails on the deck. The defining experiences of exploratory cruises come from disembarking and exploring, from the moment the anchor drops. This is the traveller's chance to go deep into enchanting environs by foot, bike, horse, Zodiac boat, kayak or even a stand-up paddleboard...

SAIL ON – SUSTAINABLY

Placing an emphasis on responsible, eco-conscious practices, many exploratory cruises enable up-close encounters with wildlife in pristine landscapes. As ambassadors from faraway lands, passengers should leave no trace of their presence behind.

THE GALÁPAGOS ISLANDS, ECUADOR
Explore the origins of Darwin's theories among the world's most unique and abundant wildlife on a Silversea (www.silversea.com) voyage around these famed, isolated islands.

THE PANTANAL, BRAZIL
Make yourself at home on a Wild Planet Adventures (www.wildplanetadventures.com) riverboat on an expedition in the heart of South America, where the verdant land is ruled by the tides.

⭷ THE KIMBERLEY, AUSTRALIA
Set sail with Zegrahm Expeditions (www.zegrahm.com) to glimpse iconic creatures – from giant crocodiles to skittish wallabies – in one of Australia's wildest regions.

ENDS OF THE EARTH

If you have a penchant for extremes, plan a cruise to the Poles. Setting sail to get there is a thrill – a sojourn to the globe's distant realms is truly all about the journey *and* the destination.

THE ARCTIC

The Arctic is a wonderland of ice-laden landscapes and extraordinary animal life. Lindblad Expeditions (www.expeditions. com) hosts several voyages, from Norway's polar bear haven of Svalbard to the Canadian High Arctic's myriad islands.

↘ ANTARCTICA

No place in the world inspires exploration like the White Continent. Wildlife is spectacular and abundant, and nature dictates all schedules. In addition to Zodiac rides, Quark Expeditions (www. quarkexpeditions.com) offers excursions such as mountaineering and ice camping.

EPIC RIVER ADVENTURES

Exploratory cruises aren't exclusive to oceans and seas – rivers are ideal for reaching remote refuges without roads, or towns and cities too far inland to reach from a seaport.

→ THE MEKONG

The Mekong is awash with flourishing nature and kaleidoscopic floating markets. Avalon Waterways (www.avalonwaterways.com) offers a spectrum of shore excursions, from visits to local villages to tours of temples.

THE NILE

Sail with Viking River Cruises (www.viking rivercruises.com) to see Egypt's many wonders. Stops range from the ancient ruins of Luxor to the famous Pyramids of Giza.

THE AMAZON

This vast river beckons wildlife-lovers with monkeys, tropical birds, sloths and more. Rainforest Cruises (www.rainforestcruises. com) has routes in Ecuador, Peru and Brazil.

DAVID MERRON © 500PX PHOTO

XUANHUONGHO © SHUTTERSTOCK

MARK READ ©LONELY PLANET IMAGES

DIVERSE DEMOGRAPHICS

There are exploratory cruises to suit anyone with a taste for adventure. Families, retirees and solo travellers of all ages will encounter a unique on-board community; some operators enable travellers to engage with local residents, too.

→ CROSS-CULTURAL EXCHANGE

Interest in Cuba is booming, and exploratory cruises here can provide opportunities for person-to-person interaction. Globus Journeys (www. globusjourneys.com) pairs sightseeing with chances to meet local business owners, musicians, farmers and baseball players.

MADE FOR MILLENNIALS

Don't fancy backpacking across Europe? Take a boat instead. In 2018, U by Uniworld (ubyuniworld.com) is offering cruises to the 21–45 set who'd rather ditch cumbersome packs in favour of hip ship cabin digs.

• By MaSovaida Morgan

CROSS-GENERATIONAL TRAVEL

Family holidays have come of age. Banish memories of tense car rides and bickering by the beach, and embrace cross-generational travel: blissfully adult trips for grown-ups and their grown-up kids.

FAMILY TRAVEL GROWS UP

This is the chance for you and your parents to kiss a fond goodbye to all those memories of teary meltdowns in hushed museums, swallowed fistfuls of sand, rows over missing Travel Scrabble tiles, or whatever else marked your early travel experiences as a family. Forgive and forget as you embrace a new, mature era of cross-generational travel. There's often a particular occasion that gets your clan on a plane together again as adults: visiting a sibling who lives

EMBRACING
THE UNEXPECTED

Travel is unpredictable, and you never know when the gods might throw a chance event or meeting in your path that makes you see your parents in a different light: when on earth did your dad acquire a taste for smoking shisha, or your mum learn to speak a little Russian? You've got time to find out the full story, because conversations that would normally be wrapped up on a quick phone-call can now drift on for days – on slow train journeys, or through long lunches that slide into dinnertime.

overseas, or attending a cousin's wedding somewhere exotic. For other families it's practical – if you're all living far apart and have busy schedules, taking shared holidays can be the only way to spend a decent amount of time together. Regardless of the initial prompt, there's no doubt that bringing your parents on holiday as an adult can add to the travel experience in ways you'd never expect.

JOHN WARBURTON-LEE © GETTY IMAGES

PONCHO © GETTY IMAGES

When people are plucked from their routines and are far from the familiar, they have the chance to shake off traditional family roles and see new sides to each other. Maybe there's a dormant competitive streak in the family, just waiting to be uncovered at the top of a black run in a Rockies ski resort. Or a shared obsession with sculpture that you didn't know about until an afternoon at Paris' Musée d'Orsay. Could a freakish willingness to eat deep-fried scorpions be buried in your bloodline? The answer might be waiting in a Bangkok side-street.

SHARING WONDERS ...AND WOES

Shared travel can also be a chance for newer additions to the tribe to get themselves deeper into the family fold: your mother and your fiancé sharing an insatiable thirst for Aperol Spritz in Milan, perhaps, or your husband and your brother equally horrified at being served instant coffee on the Nile. It's a pretty decent test of mettle, too: if your new squeeze can survive a week away with your folks, then they're probably a keeper.

As everyone who travels knows, being

Ten great places for cross-generational travel

BUDAPEST, HUNGARY
Gentle, low-key activities for all ages, such as the Castle Hill Funicular or the thermal baths.

THE NILE, EGYPT
Your mum probably still has your school project about the Pharaohs – why not see tombs and temples for real?

OAXACA, MEXICO
Wander around this gorgeously colourful city together, snacking on spicy street food.

NAPA VALLEY, USA
Now that everyone's reached legal age, share bottles of crisp chardonnay or fruity cab savs on a wine tour.

GREAT OCEAN ROAD, AUSTRALIA
Take it in turns behind the wheel (or back-seat driving) on a spectacular coastal road trip.

KERALA, INDIA
It's impossible to do anything but unwind while cruising along the backwaters of Alleppey on a houseboat.

TYROL, AUSTRIA
Great skiing for different abilities, plus après-ski where 20- to 60-somethings party side by side.

BEIJING, CHINA
Do as Chinese families do and take a day trip together to walk the Great Wall.

KENYA
A once-in-a-lifetime safari trip will be talked about for years over the dinner table.

NAPLES, ITALY
If your family realise that they have nothing in common, then simply sit back and enjoy a pizza together.

somewhere new and different can also be tough. Most trips include their fair share of disappointments, frustrations and challenges, all of which can end up as bonding experiences... or at least leave you with something to bicker over at the next family gathering. Who insisted their French was good enough to order off-menu and only succeeded in procuring a side salad and a half-dozen oysters between four, then? *Hmm*?

At its best, travel is thrilling – that's why we do it. It lights people up and shows them at their most interested, delighted and adventurous... which aren't necessarily the elements of our personalities we have a chance to share with our families.

So, after a few successful cross-generational jaunts, any negative associations with family travel might just vanish completely. Those interminable car journeys of the dim and distant past, punctuated with whining, urgent toilet stops and outbreaks of furious kicking in the back seat, will be a thing of the distant past – unless your parents really start acting up, that is.

• By Helen Elfer

PRIVATE ISLANDS FOR ALL!

The democratisation of VIP experiences has arrived.
Thanks to global improvements in travel infrastructure and
socially motivated accommodation sharing, scouting unique
adventures has become a budget-blind endeavour. So whether
you're after a perfect Instagram post or simply want to get
away from it all, private islands are tantalisingly within reach.

↗ 1 TRANG PROVINCE, THAILAND

The domain of the *chao leh* sea gypsies, Thailand's quiet southern province of Trang feels a million miles away from the hulking resorts of Phuket. Hire a colourful longtail boat and putter out to the crystalline tidewaters of Ko Kradan, the secret Emerald Cave on Ko Muk, and the claimable limestone verticals on the ultra-quiet twin islets of Ko Lao Liang.
Thailand's beaches are public property. The Trang Islands are a great target for a backpacker version of a private island experience.

→ 2 GEORGIAN BAY, ONTARIO, CANADA

North America's Great Lakes are peppered with thousands of pine-studded islands. And Canada's cottage culture has populated their lonely coves with summer homes, making full-island rentals practically commonplace. Standouts include Deepwater Island with a cosy cottage for two perched on crisp granite, and the A-frame options off the coast of Pointe au Baril.
Search for 'Georgian Bay' on accommodation marketplace sites like www.vrbo.com. Private island rentals start at around $150 per night.

3 ILET OSCAR, MARTINIQUE

The French Caribbean's laid-back rum-swigging isle of Martinique has a secret off its eastern shores: Ilet Oscar is home to a wonderfully ramshackle B&B with four breezy rooms sporting lacquered accents and encrusted shells. Rumour has it that the original owner lost the private island paradise in a card game – his loss is our gain.

Book your stay at www.iletoscar.com. Rooms start at €200 per night including breakfast; dinners are available from €60.

4 INNER HEBRIDES, SCOTLAND

Dozens of islets spread like shattered glass from the Scottish Highlands. Mile-long Torsa Island, off Oban, has a farmhouse and colony of red deer. On the motorboat ride over, travellers can chance on dolphins and seals. For something upmarket, venture to the Isle of Eriska with its *Downton* demeanour and Michelin-anointed restaurant.

Stays at the Isle of Eriska (www.eriska-hotel. co.uk) start at £195 per person. Browse www.vladi-private-islands.de for details of other Scottish island properties of note.

LESPALENIK © SHUTTERSTOCK

5 SOCIETY ISLANDS, FRENCH POLYNESIA

The go-to destination for extravagant honeymooning delivers on every ounce of hype, thanks to turquoise water and peach-pink sand so perfect it induces fits of giggles. Bora Bora is the classic option due to its shallow lagoon and overwater bungalows orbiting a turret of stone. Tetiaroa – Marlon Brando's untouched island paradise – now features ultra-luxurious villas with direct outrigger access to a sanctuary of *motus* (Polynesian mini-isles).
Escape Bora Bora's resorts for a meal at one of La Villa Mahana's seven tables; email damien@villamahana.com to reserve.

6 ZANZIBAR, TANZANIA

Anchored by fortress-like Stone Town, this archipelago elegantly flaunts its Islamic roots from the city's old engraved doors to the small dhows (Arab sailboats) floating in sheltered bays. Private-island accommodation, such as the simple suites at Chapwani or the refined thatched huts of Mnemba, blend a distinct sense of place with unbridled castaway charm.
Luxury operator andBeyond (www.andbeyond. com) arranges Mnemba Island trips along with East African safari camps, plus its other private island offering, Benguerra in Mozambique.

7 FLATEY, ICELAND

Venture far beyond the throngs of tourists around the Golden Circle to find the island of Flatey ('Flat Island' in Icelandic), one of more than 3000 seaborne crags dotting a broad westerly fjord. Only two feuding families call the island home year-round, so you'll have the grassy acre and its precious 11-room hotel largely to yourself.
Hótel Flatey (www.hotelflatey.is) is open in summer and the island is reached daily by the Baldur public ferry (www.seatours.is).

8 MALDIVES

Nine years into diminished tourism sanctions, the sinking nation is a viable DIY destination for backpacking beach enthusiasts. Pre-planning is the key to maximising the access afforded by public inter-island ferries. And deeply discounted day rates at scenic resorts help keep your coffers from draining while you're tracking down the island chain's crystal water.
Maafushi is the busiest of the local islands, but is a good activity base. Temper your private island time with a second destination like quieter Fulidhoo, accessible by a speedboat transfer.

9 CHILOÉ, CHILE

Derived from an indigenous term meaning 'the place of seagulls', Chiloé is located about halfway down Chile's 4300km-long coastline. Tourism has been rising since the inauguration of a local airport in 2012. Today the archipelago is dotted with friendly *pensiones* and unique barn-shaped churches, flanked by a backdrop of snow-capped volcanic peaks on the mainland, plus many opportunities for individual island adventures.
Tierra Chiloé (www.tierrachiloe.com) is an architectural marvel and a gastronomic pit-stop for when you end your island escape.

• By Brandon Presser

↘ 10 BELIZE BARRIER REEF

The planet's second-largest barrier reef system flanks Central America's coastline between Mexico and Honduras. Development has borrowed a construction ethos from Costa Rica, creating low-impact bungalows instead of ostentatious displays of wealth. Take over the entirety of Bird Island with a booking on Airbnb or shoot out to the far-flung Sapodilla Cayes Marine Park for rustic digs at bargain basement prices.

Reach the Sapodillas from the mainland port in Punta Gorda and hire a transfer for an overnight excursion (with a side of kayaking and snorkelling).

INDEX

PER BREIEHAGEN © GETTY IMAGES

ACKNOWLEDGEMENTS

PUBLISHED IN 2017 BY LONELY PLANET GLOBAL LIMITED

CRN 554153
www.lonelyplanet.com
978 1 78657 969 0
© Lonely Planet 2017
© Photographs as indicated 2017
Printed in Singapore

MANAGING DIRECTOR, PUBLISHING Piers Pickard
ASSOCIATE PUBLISHER Robin Barton
COMMISSIONING EDITOR Jessica Cole
ASSISTANT EDITOR Christina Webb
ART DIRECTION Daniel Di Paolo
LAYOUT DESIGNER Austin Taylor
EDITORS Anita Isalska, Nick Mee
IMAGE RESEARCHER Ceri James
CARTOGRAPHY Michael Garrett, Wayne Murphy
PRINT PRODUCTION Larissa Frost, Nigel Longuet
COVER IMAGE LucVi © Shutterstock
THANKS TO Tom Davis, Barbara Di Castro, Flora McQueen, Adam Moore, Jacob Rhoades

WRITTEN BY James Bainbridge, Oliver Berry, Joe Bindloss, Abigail Blasi, Piera Chen, Gregor Clark, Fionn Davenport, Megan Eaves, Helen Elfer, Bailey Freeman, Bridget Gleeson, Imogen Hall, Tom Hall, Alex Howard, Mark Johanson, Patrick Kinsella, Marika McAdam, AnneMarie McCarthy, Sophie McGrath, Rebecca Milner, MaSovaida Morgan, Matt Phillips, Liza Prado, Brandon Presser, Brendan Sainsbury, Regis St Louis, Ryan Ver Berkmoes, Clifton Wilkinson, Chris Zeiher, Karla Zimmerman

STAY IN TOUCH lonelyplanet.com/contact

AUSTRALIA The Malt Store, Level 3, 551 Swanston St, Carlton, Victoria 3053 03 8379 8000

IRELAND Unit E, Digital Court, The Digital Hub, Rainsford St, Dublin 8

USA 124 Linden St, Oakland, CA 94607 510 250 6400

UK 240 Blackfriars Rd, London SE1 8NW 020 3771 5100

MIX
Paper from
responsible sources
FSC www.fsc.org **FSC™ C021741**

Paper in this book is certified against the Forest Stewardship Council™ standards. FSC™ promotes environmentally responsible, socially beneficial and economically viable management of the world's forests.

MAKE IT HAPPEN

Plan your 2018 travel with Lonely Planet

New Zealand (Aotearoa)

Ethiopia & Djibouti

Portugal

Korea

Chile & Easter Island

South Africa Lesotho & Swaziland

China

Mauritius, Reunion & Seychelles

Georgia, Armenia & Azerbaijan

Malta & Gozo